~The Chicago Cubs~

OUR TEAM — OUR DREAM

A Cubs Fan's Journey into Baseball's Greatest Romance

Written and Photographed by

Tammy Lechner

Foreword by

Billy Williams

TRIUMPH
BOOKS

Triumph Books and colophon are registered trademarks of Random House, Inc.

Library of Congress Control Number: 2007932133

This book is available in quantity at special discounts for your group or organization. For further information, contact:

Triumph Books
542 South Dearborn Street
Suite 750
Chicago, Illinois 60605
(312) 939-3330
Fax (312) 663-3557

Printed in China
ISBN: 978-1-60078-070-7

Design by Kira Fulks * www.kirafulks.com
All photographs by Tammy Lechner © 2007

DEDICATION

To my family: Jack, Rose, John, and Steve, who brought the love of baseball to my heart
and shared the game with me, each in their own way, throughout my life

To every Chicago Cubs fan there ever has been, and ever will be—you are the magic behind
our team and our dream, and you keep the hope alive

To anyone who has a dream to follow, may you stay on its path, always believe in its destiny,
and appreciate every moment of the journey it becomes

ACKNOWLEDGEMENTS

Guidance, encouragement, and inspiration toward the creation and completion of this project came from many different people along the path of 15 years. I thank Jim Wilson, former director of photography at the Los Angeles Times for the initial challenge that set this project in motion and the support that rooted it during its early years.

Next, I thank the Chicago Cubs front office, players, and fans for embracing this idea and allowing me the opportunity to make it possible. Cubs executives John McDonough and Mark McGuire believed in the premise and gave it a green light in June 1992. Cubs media relations director Sharon Pannozzo approved the execution of the result by granting access to each of my visits with the Cubs in Arizona, Chicago, and on the road. Sharon was truly the lifeline of this project, and her countless nods of consent over the years enabled this book to become a reality.

Also, many talented friends and associates contributed their creative efforts to help mold and shape the direction of this book. Here I mostly thank Adrienne Helitzer, Manny Crisostomo, Christina Paine, Bill Strode, Jean Ardell, and Rich Cahan each for their creative input and ideas that helped to evolve this project along its way.

Support toward the journey itself came from many sources, and deserving special thanks for their related friendship and encouragement are Dr. Dee Fenner and Charlie Moss, Marlene and Rene Bardeau, Steve Lechner, Stephanie Leathers, Cheryl Hanson, Laura Rushing, Barbara Durell and Jon Peterson, Marlene Schneider, Stacy Davies, Catherine Boire, Suzi Chauvel, Rose Smith, Bill Swank, Jean Nieminski, Bruce Larson and Dinny Beringer, and the University of Missouri's Angus McDougall, David Reese, and Rita Reed.

To those who helped guide this project into the right hands, and ultimately deliver it into your hands, I thank Leanne Harvey, Jennifer Horseman Flowers, Julie Hill, Chuck Bailey, Jim Riordan, and Kira Fulks of Seven Locks Press, and Mitch Rogatz and the staff at Triumph Books of Chicago.

And finally, to those who lived with this "long-suffering" Cubs fan firsthand and accepted the sacrifice of time, attention, and resources I devoted to this project, I thank Adrienne, Captain, and Phoenix.

CONTENTS:

Billy Williams, a Hall of Fame outfielder, played for the Chicago Cubs from 1959–1974.
Williams returned to the Cubs after retirement as a batting instructor and coach and is a member of the Cubs executive front office today.
He is never far from the fans and he has the distinction of wearing the Cubs uniform longer than any player in the franchise's history.

BILLY WILLIAMS

This is a great story about a great team and a great dream. It reveals the secrets of an enduring love and a magical journey. It is a story passionately told by a Cubs fan. And, it is about the passion of Cubs fans. I think that's perfect, because as they say, it takes one to know one. I believe Cubs fans are the greatest in baseball. Their optimism and passion inspired me through my years in the Cubs uniform as a player and a coach. Their devotion is part of what keeps me involved with the Cubs today. Together we share a dream to witness the Cubs winning the World Series at Wrigley Field. We imagine our team charging victoriously onto the field, and Cubs fans rejoicing into the night.

This dream has lived in my mind and my heart for more than 50 years, and my hope and desire will never fade. But at the same time, when I reflect on my own journey with the Chicago Cubs I know that many of my dreams have already come true. Just being a part of this journey from season to season, and decade to decade, has been a joyful and rewarding experience in my life. It is always something to look forward to because, as this story shows, being a Cubs fan is a year-round and a lifelong commitment.

It begins early in the New Year when I join the Cubs Caravan, a tour that introduces players to the fans firsthand and gives us a chance to show our appreciation for the Cubs fans' outstanding support. The Caravan kicks off the Cubs Convention, where I enjoy meeting old and new fans and seeing good friends. The amazing energy and faith brought forward into the New Year by the thousands of Cubs fans attending this fun weekend event is uplifting. It continues in Arizona where I scout the possibilities of our team and new, young players. It's a relaxed time when I have a chance to chat with players and Cubs fans beneath the warm sunshine and remember my days as a player when Ferguson Jenkins, Ron Santo, and myself would go horseback riding through the desert. It goes into the season where opening day at Wrigley Field always brings butterflies to my stomach, as we all believe, players and fans alike, that this is our year. And it takes us on the road trips, where stadiums sell out to see the Cubs, and I have the pleasure of meeting Cubs fans who never had the chance to come to Chicago.

This story belongs to anyone who loves the Chicago Cubs. Whether as a player or a fan, this is our story of joy and pain, victory and defeat, and beyond it all, hope and faith. It's a story that needed to be told because it answers so many questions asked of us who love the Cubs and stand by this team year after year. Like the Cubs fans in this book, Tammy Lechner's passion, perseverance, and ability to document this experience is impressive. Her vision goes beyond the game of baseball to take us on an eternal journey that belongs to each of us. Not only is Tammy a great Cubs fan, but she also had the special opportunity as a professional photojournalist to be the Cubs fan who got to do more—to take us inside the scoreboard, spend the morning with the grounds crew, go to the bleachers and the rooftops, walk on the field with the ballplayers, and chat with me on the dugout bench before games to tell me about her love for the Cubs from childhood. From winter to spring to fall, through 15 seasons, through photographs and interviews, Tammy captures the very heart and spirit of baseball's greatest romance: the Chicago Cubs, their fans, and the dream we all share.

Part One

PROMISE OF A NEW YEAR

Snow had fallen on
Wrigley Field
just days earlier...
"I am waiting..." it seemed to say,
"waiting with you... waiting for you."

Wrigley Field rests beneath a fresh blanket of January snow as Cubs fans usher in the New Year,
once again looking forward to the annual Cubs Fan Convention in downtown Chicago.

CHAPTER 1

A Timeless Trance

It was a moment to stay in…to always remember. Tens of thousands of empty seats surrounded the perfect symmetry of a white diamond with waves of olive green. Snow had fallen on Wrigley Field just days earlier, purging the trials and tribulations of the past baseball season with a magical serenity. "I am waiting…," it seemed to say, "waiting with you…waiting for you."

My desire to throw arms wide open and return the embrace of this ethereal message was interrupted by the reality of my circumstance. I became intensely aware of my privilege to be in this space where millions have come and gone, laughed and cried, and inevitably, at the end of each hopeful season, pressed their undaunted hearts out like banners proclaiming, "Wait Until Next Year."

I was enchanted… Caught in a timeless trance where the present was also the past and the future, I realized that as Wrigley Field has patiently weathered nearly 100 winters, very few people get to see it dressed in white.

This made me wonder if perhaps Wrigley Field is taken for granted by those who see it often, particularly every day. At the time, I couldn't imagine such a fate. Yet, as the journey I began on this day would continue over the next 15 seasons, I came to better understand the Cubs fan's philosophy toward life… too much of a good thing isn't always good… be careful what you wish for… and of course, "Wait until next year."

Beneath these pearls of wisdom, however, there lay a mystery. How is it that, season after season, such unrequited love remains undiminished? With this question in mind I searched the quiet solitude of Wrigley Field for an answer. Looking back at me, it seemed to whisper a reply: "I know."

Winter finds Wrigley Field's ivy-coated outfield wall waiting to bloom with the season.

**Summer finds the ivy in full blossom,
alive with the energy and excitement of baseball.**

Herein lies the secret, I thought, as if gazing upon Mecca at the end of a long pilgrimage. Yet, rather than being a destination, this place would prove to be the destiny. And I would return to it many times while following Cubs fans along their path of eternal hope. Like a dream, this was a journey that would develop in its own time and reveal secrets to me in its own way. I had no clear idea where it would lead me…or when it would release me. It would become, in fact, a piece of the baseball odyssey that I joined when I became a Cubs fan nearly 30 years earlier but that existed long before me and continues on through one century and now into another. It would consist of many journeys, begun in many places, telling many stories like my own.

I was 11 years old in 1969 when the Chicago Cubs entered my life. Late summer's lazy haze was uplifted that year by a growing excitement in my small town in upstate New York as the "Amazing Mets" were about to overcome the first-place Chicago Cubs in the National League Eastern Division.

Though the Mets had the momentum of the season on their side, I decided to be contrary and root for the Cubs. That turned out to be the day a baseball romance came to me and changed my life forever. Yet, at the time I didn't realize how many "next years" awaited me. I also didn't know that I would eventually travel thousands of miles to see Wrigley Field covered with snow, sit with the bleacher bums, party in Wrigleyville, ride the trains through Chicago, take in Cubs Conventions and spring trainings, get to know Cubs players and coaches, and photograph more than 100 Cubs games at Wrigley Field and elsewhere.

But, here I was, with the field temperature a crisp 35 degrees, frozen in a private moment of regard with the Friendly Confines and contemplating the coming baseball season. With these thoughts of summer I felt a warm breeze pass over me, laced with the aroma of cold beer and smoky links. I saw the white diamond turn emerald green as the empty seats burst into a kaleidoscope of color. I heard Cubs fans singing along with Harry, whose booming voice rose above the roar of the crowd to declare, "Cubs Win!"

These were things I knew would happen, sure as the sun would rise and set. Beyond this, I could only wait for what this New Year might bring. After all, they say that one of the charming things about baseball is the fact that you just never know.

CHAPTER 2

Kindness of Strangers

**The sun sets at the Addison train
platform near Wrigley Field.**

Odd as it seemed, the middle of winter turned out to be the perfect time to begin a journey following Cubs fans. As I stepped out into the frigid air of a mid-January afternoon and headed toward the train station, I was enthralled with this rare circumstance of being in Cubs territory. And I wondered, as I often would, if the people living here appreciated their fortune as much as I did.

Arriving at the station in what I thought was plenty of time to catch the eastbound train, I just missed my ride, and the next one wouldn't be through for two hours. The ticket agent sensed my dismay. Peering at me through the steel bars of his office, he wondered aloud why I didn't know the train schedule better and where was I going with all the camera gear.

"I'm heading downtown to the Cubs Convention," I explained. Suddenly, the curiosity disappeared from his face, as if a magic word had slipped off my tongue: *Cubs.* I didn't need to go any further with my explanation. Charles O'Donnell and I were instantly bonded and he completely understood my dilemma. Within a half hour the ticket office was closed and Charles was driving me along the Eisenhower Expressway, straight to the Chicago Hilton and Towers along Michigan Avenue where the Cubs Convention was about to get under way.

Along the way, Charles told me that I would find Cubs fans to be a breed apart. "But of course," he added, "you have already found the world's greatest Cubs fan right here."

I suggested that the convention would be packed with thousands of people who also believe they are the world's greatest Cubs fans.

"Yes," Charles replied thoughtfully, "they will claim that. But, you know, they're all wrong, except me," he grinned knowingly, and then added a long chuckle before launching into his tale.

"It was 1945," he started slowly while maintaining his stare through the windshield, as if his memory stretched out on the road before him and he was following it back through time. "I was overseas for World War II, stationed in Germany. The Cubs were in the World Series against Detroit. Last World Series we've been in, you know. I didn't bet on the game because I'm not the betting type. But this fella from Detroit tells me afterward that I owe him $5.00. I said to him, 'For what?' He said, 'Because you bet on the Cubs in the Series.' Well, I told him I didn't bet, but he still swore I did and insisted I pay him. So, I gave him the $5.00 just so he wouldn't think Cubs fans are cheap."

Charles glanced toward me for a reaction and I returned a warm smile, letting him know that I appreciated his effort to single-handedly uphold the honor of Cubs fans everywhere. To commiserate, I told him that I became a Cubs fan in 1969, and he winced at mention of the year.

"The infield choked in the last two months," he declared. "They didn't make any of the plays they should have made. Oh, I cried. Well, I nearly cried."

With 44 years on the railroad, and being born and raised in Chicago, Charles noted that he has seen the city progress quite a bit…but not the Cubs. "I wish they would, by gosh," he declared, adding that "the more things change, the more they stay the same with the Cubs."

But, win or lose, he admitted that he will always root for the Cubs, though his trips to Wrigley no longer occur. Instead he takes in the games on television at a tavern in Berwyn, the next town in toward Chicago from Riverside. It's a place called the Hourglass where he gathers with other longtime Cubs fans after closing the depot ticket office each afternoon.

"We're a bunch of old timers, and boy, we were an angry group about the night games," he said with warning. "We're all from the line of thinking that baseball is to be played on the grass, under the sunshine."

Charles invited me to come to the Hourglass sometime, adding that the tavern got its name because "time may be running out on us old Cubs fans." I accepted the invitation, explaining that I planned to return during the season and would enjoy watching a game with him and his friends. On that note, I asked him what he thought the Cubs prospects were for the upcoming season.

"Oh, depends on which way the wind blows," he revealed, which is more fact than fiction as statements go about the Cubs.

The Red Line train runs from downtown to Wrigley Field.

CHAPTER 3

Conventioneers in Cubdom

And so, through the kindness of a Cubs fan I made it to my first Cubs Convention on time. Meanwhile, Cubs fans drove in from Wisconsin, Iowa, Indiana, and downstate Illinois, and flew in from states stretching to the far corners of the nation. They came from cities, suburbs, small towns, and farms. With them they brought a passion that always has been and always will be.

With all things past forgiven, and all things yet to come accepted, the annual Cubs Convention is one of the ways to endure being a Cubs fan. It comes along a few weeks after the holidays and several weeks before spring training, or right about the time when most avid baseball fans are singing the off-season blues. Those who attend say it offers fun, friendship, and the opportunity to celebrate the promise of a New Year.

For three action-packed days the convention transforms a downtown Chicago hotel into a Wrigley Field made up of carpet, marble, brass, and fluorescent lighting. Opening day finds bellhops hustling like ushers to bring a crowd of about 15,000 anxious Cubs fans together for a party that includes former and current players, coaches, managers, and front-office personnel.

For most, the first order of business is to do a quick scan of the weekend agenda to see who is doing what, when, and where. This translates into how to rub elbows with your favorite Cubs during autograph and photo sessions; fielding, pitching, and batting clinics; panel discussions; question-and-answer seminars; and trivia games. Meanwhile, the lower level of the hotel offers a square country mile of exhibit halls displaying under one roof all the Cubs memorabilia in the universe ever for sale.

Bellhops hustle with luggage from Cubs fans descending upon the Chicago Hilton & Towers where the Cubs Fans Convention takes place early in the New Year. The event transforms the hotel into a baseball paradise during an action-packed weekend featuring former and current Cubs players, drawing more than 15,000 Cubs fans from near and far.

A frenzy of excited Cubs fans gather in the hotel's main ballroom to applaud the formal introduction of the Chicago Cubs team for the upcoming season. Meeting the full roster of players during the Convention's opening ceremonies kicks off the weekend's activities, and fans consider the evening a "not to be missed" highlight event. Calling the evening "a huge pep rally," the players say it gets them excited to put on the uniform and play baseball again after the long winter hiatus between seasons.

THEY CAME FROM CITIES, SMALL TOWNS, AND FARMS.
WITH THEM THEY BROUGHT A PASSION THAT ALWAYS HAS BEEN AND ALWAYS WILL BE...
IT SEEMED A TREMENDOUS RESPONSIBILITY TO REPRESENT THE DREAM
AND THE REALITY OF MILLIONS OF CUBS FANS.

Eleanor Nadr, Evelyne Kratochuill, Elanor Kaplan, and Lola Kuta have attended every Cubs Fan Convention since it began in 1986.
Shown here wearing T-shirts from a past convention and their trademark pork pie Cubs hats, the women have enjoyed a baseball
friendship all their lives. Growing up and still living in the Berwyn-Stickney area of the city's western suburbs,
they've been taking the train to Wrigley Field for Cubs games since age five.

THOSE WHO ATTEND SAY IT OFFERS FUN, FRIENDSHIP,
AND THE OPPORTUNITY TO CELEBRATE THE PROMISE OF A NEW YEAR.

With the convention barely off the ground, the mania of activity reached a crescendo when the Chicago Cubs themselves, the players who would take the field when umpires declare 'Play ball!' in the spring, made an appearance in the main ballroom. Here, to the cheers of wall-to-wall Cubs fans, the convention formally kicked off.

"Ladies and Gentlemen," bellowed Cubs public address announcer Wayne Messmer after calling the final player out to the lineup, "your Chicago Cubs!"

A thunderous roar swelled to fill the spacious ballroom. It seemed a tremendous responsibility, I thought, as the standing-room-only ovation continued, to represent the dream—and the reality—of millions of Cubs fans.

The pep rally gained even greater momentum as Messmer introduced Cubs legends and heroes of the past. The crowd's reception for these former players made it clear that a Cub is a Cub…forever.

Rolland Rapp of Speer, Illinois, hurries toward an autograph session with a Cubs player fully outfitted in his own Cubbies paraphernalia. There proves to be something for everyone at the convention, from young to old fans, and former to new players. Yet, year after year, the main attraction of the convention is the fans themselves. (Left)

Cubs fans Laverne and Larry Wendorf of Elmwood Park, Illinois, put a stitch into a Cubs logo quilt being created on-site at the convention by nationally renowned quiltmaker Barbara Dannenfelser of New Jersey. Each fan donated one dollar to the Chicago Cubs charity, Cubs Care, for the opportunity to make their own "stitch in time." (Right)

Like the ballplayers lined up on the ballroom balcony, I, too, felt captivated by the overwhelming emotion of this crowd of true-blue Cubs fans. How I had longed to be on the majority end of a crowd cheering on their team.

After all, for me it was lonely growing up as a Cubs fan in New York's Hudson Valley. In fact, it didn't even seem possible that somewhere there were millions of Cubs fans in one place. To me Chicago seemed as far away and fictional as the Emerald City.

Jack Keeley was the only other Cubs fan I knew through my formative years. He wrote a sports column for our town's newspaper. My father, who played softball as if it were one of life's rites of passage, knew Keeley well and introduced me to him so I would know that I wasn't the only person in New York crazy enough to claim being a Cubs fan. I asked Keeley if he knew where I could buy a Cubs cap, and he quickly scribbled an address on a scrap of paper and handed it to me.

"You can actually write to the Cubs?" I questioned, stunned that this place, Wrigley Field, was reachable in any way—by mail, phone, car, or plane.

"Yes," Keeley assured me. "You just write a nice note to them and ask for a merchandise catalog. They'll send it to you, and then you can order that cap."

Without delay, I took out my lined notebook paper and pencil to carefully craft a letter to the Cubs at Wrigley Field and request my catalog. "Dear Sir...," I'm sure it started. I remember wondering if they wouldn't mind sending a catalog to someone all the way in New York.

Now, here I was, surrounded by thousands of Cubs fans wearing thousands of Cubs caps. I realized that, despite the lack of a baseball field, I had arrived in Cubdom, a place where saying you are a Cubs fan is a verbal passport to the most heartfelt fraternity. It is an association that allows you to connect and belong. It opens doors, hearts, and memories. It is a bonding unlike any other in the world of sports, and with this one thing in common anything becomes possible.

Harry Caray served as the honorary chairman of the Cubs Fan Convention through 12 years, and always commanded one of the longest lines of autograph seekers. Harry's popularity at the convention was so overwhelming that the Cubs devised a lottery drawing allowing a certain number of fans specific time slots to meet with him. A baseball bearing Harry Caray's classic "Holy Cow" signature is proudly displayed by a Cubs fan willing to wait her turn for a personal moment with the legendary broadcaster.

Part Two

HOPE SPRINGS ETERNAL

SOMEHOW I KNEW... THAT MANY JOYFUL SURPRISES AWAITED ME...

As Cubs players sprint off the line to begin their spring training, Buzzy Labno of Chicago shows the overwhelming excitement of Cubs fans arriving in the warm Arizona sunshine to take in the pre-season experience and catch a few autographs along the way. For Cubs fans of all ages, the balmy breeze of spring renews hope for the upcoming season.

CHAPTER 4

Warm Possibilities

It was hard to imagine, while driving through the Sonora Desert, that the spring-training home of the Chicago Cubs would appear "just around the corner." In fact, it was hard to imagine anything beyond saguaro cactus and sagebrush, as the vast desert landscape seemed infinite. Yet, with Interstate 10 stretching forward in a perfectly straight line between Los Angeles and Phoenix, the concerns of yesterday faded as memories of a long winter were left behind, and the Superstition Mountains of Phoenix finally come into view. I consider all the different pilgrimages being made by Cubs fans like myself to this place called the Valley of the Sun. I imagine suitcases being packed under the gray and dreary skies of a Chicago winter day, trading out long johns for shorts, wool socks for tank tops, and leaving heavy winter coats in the closet. Arizona locals call them "snow birds," flocking to this spring-training ritual more than a million strong each year to feel the warm possibility of October in the fresh breeze of spring. After a long winter hiatus I could hear them proclaiming, "It's time for baseball."

Somehow I knew, as I approached the Cubs spring-training complex in Mesa, that many joyful surprises awaited me. Before I even had time to get my bearings, a bright and cheerful 30-year-old woman approached me. Donning a Cubs hat atop an already well-tanned face she wanted to know all about me. As I stated my purpose for existing I noticed a unique pin on the side of her cap, but couldn't quite make out the logo.

A small opening in the tarp surrounding the Cubs practice fields at Fitch Park in Mesa, Arizona,
provides a peephole for watching the team's morning exercise drills to a passerby.
With lots of new names showing up on Cubs uniforms in the beginning of spring training, fans get an early
preview of how the team shapes up for the new campaign.

"It's time for baseball," point out Cubs fans fully attired in their favorite Cubs hat, jacket, and jersey while flocking to Arizona as part of a spring training audience totaling more than a million strong.

"It's time for baseball!"

"The pin says ' IF IT TAKES FOREVER...," Janet Strejc stated, and then added, "And you know, I guess it has.... I mean I suppose it could.... But what does it matter?"

"It...," I replied back to Janet. "What is it?" I decided to ask just to see what she would say, though I already knew that it was the reason I was there. She went on to explain that in a literal sense it means the many decades of waiting for the Cubs to win a second World Series. But, in a more figurative sense, it refers to the endless hope and unwavering devotion of Cubs fans and the fun that comes along while they wait.

Janet tells me that when her family moved from Chicago to Arizona in her late teens, she became hooked on the spring-training season. "Though as a kid in Chicago I never cared much about spring training. I thought, big deal, they're not ready yet. But when we moved away this became my chance to see the Cubs. You can call me a spring-training junkie I guess." She adds that she takes all her vacation time, from her job as a grocery checker, for spring training, and mostly enjoys getting to know other Cubs fans. Her favorite is Doris Davis, a retired professor from Indiana. Within a few strides Doris is found, with eyes trained intently on the players laboring through stretches and sprints.

Doris shares that she's been coming to spring training since retiring from teaching at the University of Wisconsin in 1980. When she tells me that she believes she is the number one Cubs fan my thoughts trail back to my talk with Charles O'Donnell as he drove me to the Cubs Convention a month earlier. We had agreed that I would meet many people claiming to be the greatest Cubs fan.

As I tune back in to Doris I hear her next remark echo my memory. "Well, I know a lot of people claim that. But I've been a Cubs fan since I was a little girl. My dad passed it on to me.

With the morning sun warming their backs, the fans line up above the Cubs dugout at Ho-Ho-Kam Stadium
to watch an inter-squad practice on the field and show support to their boys in blue.

He'd get out a checkerboard and we'd make yellow the Cubs and black the other team. We'd paste names onto the pieces by using the edges of envelope flaps because Scotch tape hadn't been invented yet. Then, while my dad was at work I would listen to the game on the radio, and I'd arrange the checkers to show him what happened when he got home. I got to know all the players."

Doris recounts her tale of becoming a Cubs fan while holding a media guide in her hand detailing the upcoming season. "I still study the players," she says. "And I also enjoy meeting other fans, so I don't mind coming alone. You'll see that there are no strangers among Cubs fans. We're all friends because we're all a part of it."

"It...," I say to myself as I move along to get a few photos of the players now finishing up the morning workout.

CALL THEM "SNOW BIRDS," FLOCKING TO THIS SPRING TRAINING RITUAL TO FEEL THE WARM POSSIBILITY OF OCTOBER IN THE FRESH BREEZE OF SPRING.

Cubs fans remembering the great Chicago Cubs team of 1969 get to share memories of a bygone era with the legendary Mr. Cub, Ernie Banks, as spring training affords a relaxed time to chat with players, former and current, as well as infamous and yet unknown.

Around the grueling workouts and practice sessions, spring training is a fun time for players as well as fans. Here, Cubs first baseman Mark Grace shares a laugh with his teammates during the morning stretching exercises.

Three young women from Wisconsin's Marquette University visiting Arizona during spring
break. From left are Heather Todd, Amy Manderscheid, and Elizabeth Sobczak.

We had agreed that I would meet many people claiming to be the greatest Cubs fan.

Acquiring an autograph from Ryne Sandberg was a quest for Cubs fans during the superstar second baseman's tenure with the team. While some fans, such as Stosh, politely request his signature with a sign, others find a way to climb the outfield fence and perch above him.

Catching Sandberg in the parking lot on his way home was a popular option,
and one no longer available as players now have a secured lot for parking.

CHAPTER 5

Everyone Is a Contender

Cubs coach Marty DeMerritt protects his sensitive skin from the hot desert sun with a thick layer of sunscreen as he surveys the progress of young Cubs prospects during a workout.

As I approach the Cubs practice fields at Fitch Park to photograph the day's workouts and drills, the sounds of baseball fill the warm desert air replete with an intoxicating aroma of freshly cut green grass. The moment becomes one in which I cannot imagine anything being more exciting or meaningful. Baseball has returned from its long winter's nap, purged of yesterday and full of hope for tomorrow. With this annual renewal comes an unblemished season offering promise and reward that heightens the senses and causes optimism to abound. It's a time of transition when every team is in contention, a rookie might have a shot at a veteran, and an unknown can become known.

The first days of spring training begin an essential agenda—str-e-e-e-eching and stre-e-e-engthing exercises, long hours in the batting and pitching cages, repeated drills of basic fundamentals. As I move from field to field, intent on capturing this ballet of calisthenics on film, I become aware of the hard work involved in preparing for a 162-game baseball season. I find this intensity of effort inspiring from my own standpoint: as you sow, so you shall reap. A formula begins to develop in my psyche: preparation, passion, persistence, patience, and prayer.

While the majority of Cubs fans show up later for the March games, some prefer the more casual atmosphere of the early practice schedule. Toting backpacks surely containing water bottles and sunscreen these early arrivers create a colorful audience, each outfitted in something that says "Cubs," from a simple ball cap to shoelaces. With brimming enthusiasm they follow the players through their drills, studying the roster card to learn who the new kids in camp are while waiting anxiously for the chance to have a precious piece of memorabilia autographed by a renowned favorite.

Cubs manager Don Baylor seems to beckon strength from the sun's rays as he sets an example of team leadership by sweating his way through the practice along with his players.

For young players, like outfielder Roosevelt Brown, spring training is their first opportunity to impress major league coaches.

BASEBALL HAS RETURNED FROM ITS LONG WINTER NAP, PURGED OF YESTERDAY AND FULL OF HOPE FOR TOMORROW.

Many fans who show up early are either Chicago natives transplanted to retirement in Phoenix, or native Arizonans who have grown to love the Cubs through the team's annual visit to Mesa. Mary Marmas's home is just a block away and right near Ho-Ho-Kam Park, where the Cubs play their spring games. "This is our Wrigley Field West," she comments while taking a break from getting snapshots of her son, Matt, collecting autographs. "I enjoy bringing both my son and daughter here because I think baseball is a good activity for them. Each year they pick favorite players during the spring, collect autographs, and then follow them through the season," she notes, emphasizing that the kids call the players "Mister" or "Sir," and always ask "may I please," and follow up with a sincere "thank you." "As a parent I like to come and watch them interact, and I want to take a few pictures of my own," she winks at me with a nod toward my gear hanging off my torso.

Nearby, Melvin Bunton and his wife, Gerry, say they are "hooked on coming down" to Arizona, and make the trek every year from their home in Morris, Illinois. They spend three weeks in Mesa and then continue on to visit relatives in Las Vegas and California. As we talk Gerry spots me noticing the logo on her T-shirt, "IF IT TAKES FOREVER…" Pointing at the phrase she says the Cubs always win when she wears the shirt. "I don't know what I'll do when it wears out," she remarks. I suggest she save it for later in the year, when the games count. "Good idea," she agrees. "I'll save it for October then."

While physical conditioning is the main focus of spring training, mental preparation and the seeding of team chemistry are also of valued importance. In the spring of 2001 the Cubs took a bold step to hire a fitness guru, Mack Newton, to take the whole concept of conditioning to a higher level: body, mind, and spirit. Equipped with a microphone for intensifying the urgency of his message, Newton marches like a drill sergeant through the rows of Cubs players to impart the philosophy of "performance."

"You're in the process of getting in shape," he barks at them, "but this is just the beginning, and it's the easy part. Because we're not here to prepare for just 162 games. We're here to prepare for 18 more games in October. So when you begin to get tired I want you to think of playing baseball in October. Tired? Think of October! Does it hurt? Think of October!"

"You are always either becoming better or worse," continues Newton. "There's no such thing as maintaining. So do not ever think you've reached success, because once you think that you are done! Let go of the past—last year is LAST YEAR!"

WHILE PHYSICAL-CONDITIONING IS THE MAIN FOCUS OF SPRING TRAINING, MENTAL PREPARATION AND THE SEEDING OF TEAM CHEMISTRY ARE ALSO OF VALUED IMPORTANCE.

Conditioning expert Mack Newton uses a microphone to bark encouragement at Cubs players with a goal of motivating them to reach 100 percent, getting into the best possible shape for the long season ahead.

CHAPTER 6

King of the Cactus League

"The Diamondbacks may live here, but the Cubs own this town," said Cubs former manager Dusty Baker, remarking on the fact that the Chicago Cubs popularity in Arizona's spring season outstrips Phoenix's hometown team. Even for fans devoted to other teams, such as the Giants or the Angels, a trip to Arizona generally includes seeing the Cubs.

Yet, fans visiting the spring-training home of the Cubs in Mesa for the first time cannot help but wonder exactly how the stadium came to be named Ho-Ho-Kam, and who are all these helpful guys running about in red shirts adorned with turquoise jeweled bolos, also known as the Ho-Ho-Kams.

The name is from an Indian tribe, the Ho-Ho-Kams, who called the Salt River Valley home centuries ago. In the spring of 1951 the same name anointed a special events committee, born as an arm of the Mesa Chamber of Commerce with the philanthropic goal of aiding the community through special projects. Led by Dwight Patterson, a Mesa rancher and one among six of the founding members, the Ho-Ho-Kams were determined in the early going to bring major league spring baseball to Mesa.

The big break came when the New York Giants decided to swap Florida for Arizona as a spring-training site. At the same time, Patterson learned that Cubs owner Phil Wrigley was no longer enchanted with isolating his Cubs' spring training on Catalina Island off the coast of Southern California. When the Cubs came to Arizona in the spring of 1951 to play an exhibition game with the Giants, Patterson met with Cubs officials and toured them through Rendezvous Park, built in the 1930s as a WPA project. The park was barely sufficient as a baseball site, but the Cubs agreed to share the cost of stadium improvements with the City of Mesa. And so it was that Arizona's Cactus League was formed between the Cubs and Giants.

Dwight W. Patterson is considered the founding father of Arizona's Cactus League, which offers major league teams training facilities, stadiums, and competitive games during the preseason.

The Cubs stadium in Mesa is named after Patterson, and the city's philanthropic arm of its Chamber of Commerce, the Ho-Ho-Kams. The stadium, which received a makeover in 1997, is managed and operated by the Ho-Ho-Kam organization.

Always a venue packed full of Cubs fans, Ho-Ho-Kam Stadium, as shown above, drew about 9,000 fans until a renovation in 1997 brought the seating capacity up to about 12,500. The upgrades included a face lift to the field and the facility, shown at right, where the Ho-Ho-Kam members run the show on game days.

The Ho-Ho-Kams and the Cubs would see record attendance for spring training in the future, along with revenues that poured money into Mesa's Youth Sports Programs. In 1984 the Cubs became the first major league team to draw more than 100,000 fans in its home schedule, and the Cactus League today draws more than a million baseball fans to Arizona each spring. The Ho-Ho-Kams operate the facility in cooperation with the Cubs and claim that "it's safe to say the Cubs are the toughest ticket in the Valley every spring."

A face-lift to Ho-Ho-Kam Park in 1997 brought the stadium's seating capacity up from about 9,000 to 12,500 and added upgrades such as an electronic scoreboard above a spacious grass berm and an internal concourse offering improved concessions.

A rare rainy day greeted the ballpark's inaugural day, but the weather didn't damper the enthusiasm of Cubs fans who lined up as early as 10:30 AM to buy tickets for the 1:00 PM game. Among the early birds was Jim Mozingo, a U.S. Marine stationed in Okinawa, Japan, who timed his vacation with spring training so he could visit Mesa and the Cubs. He flew 20 hours from Japan to San Diego where he picked up his wife and two young daughters and then drove another six hours to Mesa.

"I grew up on a farm in Burwick, Illinois," he said. "When we were out in the fields working, all we had to listen to on our radios was WGN and the Cubs. But I think the whole town of 200 people, along with my graduating class of 31 kids, were all Cubs fans. I remember a lot of fun times going to Peoria with my friends to see Mark Grace play as a minor leaguer."

After Jim joined the military he was stationed in San Diego and went to every Cubs versus Padres game. "My uncle, Ralph Cannon, pitched for the Pittsburgh Pirates," he said, "so I've always been very connected to the game. In fact, my uncle brought me here to Ho-Ho-Kam in 1979, and I remember that was the first season of the old Rendezvous Park being renovated to become Ho-Ho-Kam. And now here I am again to see a new park once more, but with the same name this time."

Mozingo and the other 8,800-plus fans in attendance that day saw the Cubs bless the new park with a movie-script perfect 6–2 win over the Seattle Mariners. Ryne Sandberg hit the first homer over the wall with Sammy Sosa to follow. The view of the Superstitious Mountain range was spectacular, noted the fans, with Red Mountain jutting above the 80-foot-tall green "batter's eye" in center field, and snow covered Four Peaks sparkling beyond right field.

"The only thing that could have been better was having more sun," commented Sandberg in a postgame radio interview with former Cubs great and now broadcaster Ron Santo.

"Well, Billy Williams and myself sure wish we had something like this during our spring days here," Santo remarked back. "At old Rendezvous Park all we had was a playing field, one extra practice field, and a couple of pitching machines. We had to stay a long time after games and wait our turns to get in all of our work."

With the upgrades the new Ho-Ho-Kam Stadium and Fitch Park training complex was being billed as the "jewel" of the Cactus League, featuring the traditional stucco finish of Southwest architecture and sporting steel trusses and a steel canopy above the upper deck to give it that "old ballpark" feel popular with more recent stadium designs. And it cemented a Mesa union with the Cubs for another 20 years. The only complaints I heard from Cubs fans that day were "Where's the bratwurst?" and "Couldn't this have more of a Chicago atmosphere?" My response to them was, "Hey, like they say in France, Vive la difference!"

Wearing their own special uniforms Ho-Ho-Kam members get involved in everything from selling tickets, to parking cars as well as ushering fans to seats and providing concessions. After the game a group of Ho-Ho-Kams get together for a game of cards in the break room (left) to celebrate a job well done.

CHAPTER 7

Are We Ready Yet?

With the first two weeks of training completed, tendons stretched, and biceps strengthened, the calendar flipped to March to let the games begin. In the days leading up to the beginning of the 30-plus spring game schedule I noticed the crowd thickening and parking spaces tougher to spot at the Fitch Park complex. As the energy of newcomers quickened the pace, those of us who came early felt a loss for the relaxed yesterdays. But on the official opening day, an atmosphere of swirling excitement greeted me upon my arrival to Ho-Ho-Kam Park, and I was mindful that the game of baseball was why we were all there. It was time to play ball!

Although the games of spring training do not count, they are a critical prelude to the real deal—now just 30 days away. Vital evaluations and decisions are made during these games regarding performance and player selection. As the games of March unfold, the expanded roster shrinks until only 25 men head north as the Chicago Cubs. The remainder are either sent back to the minor leagues or cut loose. For a rookie player this might be the only opportunity to impress the manager and his coaching staff. For a veteran player at the end of the road, this also translates into a time to prove you've still got it.

These games are exhilarating for the fans because they get to see their team take the field after a five-month absence. Even Ballpark Dave, one of the crown princes of Wrigley Field's "ballhawks," comes to Mesa to hoist the Dominican flag as he does on Chicago's Waveland Avenue as a salute to Sammy Sosa's home runs. "But," the Cubs ask him, "can you fly that flag beneath the American flag?" After all, even Sammy Sosa says, "God Bless America."

Charlie Gorski of Champaign, Illinois, gets a kick out of watching Cubs pitcher Turk Wendell employing superstition by jumping over the foul line (left), while Cubs fans get a kick out of Charlie's game hat, designed by his grandmother and embellished with pins donated by various Cubs fans over the seasons.

As I approached the media gate to pick up my credential for photographing the game I heard a Cubs fan say, "This is going to be the year." I was immediately swept into their wave of supercharged energy and unbridled enthusiasm. They dashed toward the stadium seats as if they could be the first one to claim a pot of gold.

I realized I better follow as I suddenly felt like I was missing something, too. While trying to make my own bee-line to the field I passed the batting cages and spotted Suzanne Rogers holding up her toddler for a better view of the players inside, practicing during the final hour leading up to the game. Dressed in a white-and-blue-striped baseball outfit that says "Pro" on the back, 14-month-old Ryne Rogers was named after Cubs second baseman Ryne Sandberg, explained Suzanne. "His grandfather wanted him named after him, which would be Bernard," said Suzanne, "and we said no way. Sandberg is our favorite player, so we decided to go with Ryne."

I share that Sandberg is one of my favorites, too, and I suspect I'll be meeting more children born into the world bearing the names of Cubs players. I smile at the thought of triplets being named Tinker, Evers, and Chance, after the infamous Cubs trio from the early 1900s.

The game that day was sold out, and as I climbed the long stairs to find a place behind the top row, I gained attention because of my cameras and long telephoto lenses. "Hey, don't you want to be down on the field near the players?" asked a Cubs fan. "No," I replied, "I want to be up here near you. Tell

Ruth and Paul Knoke of Phoenix, Arizona, wear their special Cubs jerseys to a spring training game. The shirts were gifts from their children for Mother's Day and Father's Day.

As Cubs catcher Rick Wilkens takes a late swing at a fast ball, he knows that the focus of spring training games is about tuning up the mechanics of your game, not so much about winning the game. Yet, a good effort deserves a hand slap and helps to build camaraderie between players and brew the chemistry so necessary to delivering a championship team in late October.

me, who are you and why are you here? And I promise I'll tell you all about me later." Jack Webber agreed and offered to buy me a beer, which I wisely declined. He began by telling me that this day was special to him because it was the first time he felt happiness since his wife died months earlier. To help him through his mourning, and to celebrate his 70th birthday, Jack's six children pitched in on a trip to Arizona for him to see the Cubs. Accompanied by his son Michael and a grin from ear-to-ear, Jack swore to me as we talked that I was the first person to bring a smile to his face in a long time. I believe what he said to be true, but as I surveyed the sellout crowd of thousands of rapturous Cubs fans, I knew Jack Webber's smile had only just begun its comeback. With that thought, the crowd roared and Jack excitedly spun around to inform me, "Sandberg just hit a homer! By God, this is going to be the year."

Spring Breaks

The accusation that Cubs fans do not care whether their team wins or loses is simply not true. Yet, spring training does encourage fans to evaluate the game based on individual performances rather than on the final score. And Cubs fans are more than happy to recite the baseball adage: "Winning spring-training games a season does not make." Besides, once the score is final, win or lose, everyone's attention turns to what fun comes next.

All around I heard players and fans alike making plans for the evening. Details on everything from tee times for a quick round of nine to dinner reservations were exchanged. "It's a great time to share with your family," the players will tell you, adding that family time is something that goes on the shelf once the bell rings to start the long season.

It's also a great time for camaraderie, says former Cubs coach and Hall-of-Fame outfielder Billy Williams. He shares that his memories of spring training seasons past include learning to ride horseback in the desert with Ron Santo and Ferguson Jenkins, both expert riders. For others golf is the ticket. The Valley of the Sun offers more than 250 courses, with the lush Mesa Country Club a favorite of Cubs players, and is nicely located just down the road from Ho-Ho-Kam Park. And for dinner after the ballgame the choices are plenty.

Yet Mesa is not the only place where the Chicago Cubs have left their footprints. Before coming to Arizona in 1952, the team gathered for spring training on Catalina Island for 30 years. "Of course I remember Catalina Island," quipped Cubs clubhouse manager Yosh Kiwana, as I cautiously interrupted his office work to ask if I could visit with him for a few minutes and talk about spring trainings of yesteryear. "Wasn't I the guy who had to load all the equipment on the boats for the trip to the island?" he asked me, as if I had been there, too.

Yosh, whom I found that day at Ho-Ho-Kam shuffling through piles of documents detailing new equipment orders and deliveries, is known to be as reticent as he is diminutive. A bit of an enigma, I approached Yosh forewarned by others in the media that "no one knows more about the Cubs but tells less than Yosh." In fact, Yosh is considered to be part of the Cubs folklore itself, as the story goes that he came to the Cubs in 1943, and

A welcome change of pace and atmosphere to the arduous regular season, spring training allows players, coaches, and managers to enjoy a relaxed atmosphere where they can spend time with family and friends and get to know their fans. Cubs manager Jim Lefevre gets a congratulatory hug from his daughter at the Cubs dugout after a game, while Cubs pitcher Greg Hibbard enjoys time at a Mesa driving range with his toddler son.

THE PLAYERS WILL TELL YOU THAT
FAMILY TIME IS SOMETHING THAT
GOES ON THE SHELF ONCE THE BELL
RINGS TO START THE LONG SEASON.

With practice over for the day and his media interviews behind him,
Cubs manager Dusty Baker grabs a handful of baseballs and heads
back to the field to throw batting practice to his young son,
Darren, and his nephew.

While waiting for his turn at bat, Darren enjoys another perfect
spring pastime—making soap bubbles float through the air. (Right)

when William Wrigley Jr. sold the Cubs to the Tribune Company in 1981, it was written into the contract that Yosh Kiwana would have a lifetime job.

His willingness to reminisce about Catalina Island was brief, but his memory was poignant as he described the magnificent Wrigley mansion perched high on a bluff overlooking Avalon Harbor and the coastline of California. The Cubs ball field was located directly beneath the bluff, and Wrigley could watch the games from the mansion's porch. Wrigley, whose ownership of the Cubs began in 1916, bought Catalina Island in 1919 for about $3 million. In 1975 the Wrigley family ceded 86 percent of the island to a land conservancy.

"Those were the good old days," said Yosh, "but it was a little inconvenient. Beyond everything having to be hauled in by boat there really wasn't anything to do there. The island had just a few places to go out." Yosh explained that after the first couple of weeks the team would sail for Los Angeles to play exhibition games at L.A.'s Wrigley Field, the home park of the Los Angeles Angels, the Pacific Coast League farm team of the Cubs, and also owned by Wrigley.

"Hey, nice talking with you, thanks for dropping in," he said, abruptly ending the short conversation. "But I've got this year to think about now. In the next two days I have to have all this equipment shipped to Chicago. Opening Day is next week. I'm up to my eyeballs in it and dealing with 25 guys who can't find their socks."

Before I left I asked Yosh if he thought this might be the year. "Oh, it's every year," he replied. "Last year becomes this year, and then it becomes next year. Believe me, it's a routine. I know," he assured me, "I've been doing this for a while."

Always a major attraction, broadcaster Harry Caray gets pulled into a family photo with a group of Cubs fans after a game at Ho-Ho-Kam Stadium.

A good fit with the relaxed and fun atmosphere of spring training, Caray celebrates his March 1 birthday in the media lounge with Cubs front office personnel and members of the Ho-Ho-Kam organization.

As Cubs clubhouse manager Yosh Kiwana checks the inventory of equipment being shipped from Mesa to Chicago in preparation for the season just days away, he recalls memories of spring seasons past, when the Cubs trained on Catalina Island, California. Visitors to Catalina Island today find that the field is now a golf course, but a plaque located nearby confirms the 30-year rendezvous between the Cubs and Catalina Island.

Louise Wise of Mesa, Arizona, proudly decorates her Mesa hair salon with Cubs photographs and memorabilia.
She and her husband Bob are like many native and year-round residents of the community who became die-hard
Cubs fans through following the team's spring seasons in Arizona. Louise is known to always have the Cubs games
on TV in her salon, and the couple's vacations always include trips to Chicago and Wrigley Field.

Part Three

CHASING THE DREAM

A BASEBALL SEASON NEVER REALLY BEGINS OR ENDS,
BUT RATHER IT CHASES YESTERDAY LIKE THE DAWN.

Wrigley Field welcomes Cubs fans like Carmella Hartigan (left) back to the ballpark on Opening Day as the game day flags are hoisted into place around the stadium's marquis at the corner of Clark and Addison Streets. Hartigan, wearing a 1908 Cubs Championship T-shirt, was six-years old when the Cubs won their last World Series.

Chapter 9

Opening Daze

"Opening Day is like your birthday, Christmas, and New Year's all rolled into one," once remarked Cubs broadcaster Chip Caray, grandson of the legendary Harry Caray, as he attempted to describe the euphoric delirium surrounding the first day of the baseball season. And certainly all baseball fans will agree that Opening Day does hold magic not offered on any other day of the year.

Yet, as I rode the train toward Wrigley Field to discover Opening Day for myself, I realized that a baseball season never really begins or ends, but rather it chases yesterday like the dawn. With the El whisking me through neighborhoods collectively known as the City of Big Shoulders, I became aware of the weight held by a passing century now pressing down on tomorrow's expectations. Approaching the Addison Street station I recognized the embodiment of this promise as Wrigley Field's rooftop became visible, and I considered that every Cubs fan has his or her own special relationship with this ballpark, his or her own litany of memories.

Welcome to Opening Day! More than three hours remained before game time, but fans were quickly lining up at Gate F, ready to burst ahead the moment the ticket turnstile swung forward. Wrigleyville was already filled with people dancing to impromptu music supplied by sax and bongo players meandering through the thickening crowd. As I headed down Waveland Avenue a raucous group dressed like the Blues Brothers was on the run with high fives for everyone. I spotted another circle of fans performing a toast, and they beckoned me to join their ritual intended to bring luck to the Cubs. They explained they do this every year in the same location with a bottle of Drambuie, Scottish liquor created in 1845 bearing a label proclaiming "The Link to '45," in hopes of linking their toast to the Cubs' last World Series appearance of 1945.

Early arrivals to Opening Day head toward Wrigley Field from the nearby Addison Street train station, fully wrapped up for a cold day in blankets, jackets, and knit caps. Yet, the often frigid temperatures that welcome baseball back to Chicago do not dampen the spirit of Cubs fans looking forward to the unveiling of another great season.

Inside Wrigley Field it takes three young men to push a dolly of beverages
up the concourse ramp to a higher field level as the stadium has few elevators.

A concession worker busily prepares ahead of time for an Opening Day crowd of
more than 40,000 hungry Cubs fans by stocking up reserves of bagged popcorn.

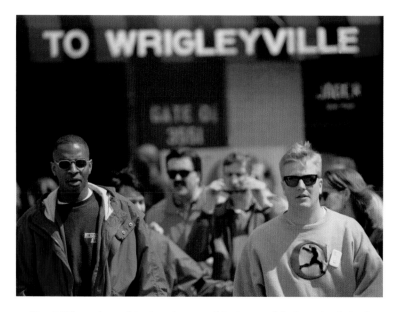

Jim Wilson loved to toast a good bet... couldn't resist it in fact. I even think that's how he measured me up when he hired me to join the photo staff of the Los Angeles Times in 1987. As director of photography of a talented and eclectic group, Wilson had a knack for placing odds in favor of blossoming potential. It was only fitting, he said, that I would turn out to be a Cubs fan. Every spring I'd find a wager voucher from Las Vegas in my assignment slot showing that Wilson put money on the Cubs for me.

In 1989 Wilson encouraged me to pursue a photo documentary project on minor league baseball in California that ended up spanning six seasons and became my first book. He liked the effort enough to challenge me to try to capture the same magic of baseball on the major league level. And so Wilson summoned me—go out there and find that magic with the Cubs!

"Boy, it's a cold day for baseball," said Betty McMillan, whom I encountered seated along the third-base line meticulously keep-ing score of the Opening Day game. "Aren't you just frozen? Would you like some hot tea?" she asked and pointed toward a thermos next to her. The reaction of the crowd stole her attention as she winced over a double play that just ended a Cubs rally. "I feel a little rusty with my score keeping," she admitted, "but like the Cubs, I suspect I'll get the hang of it again as the season goes on."

Betty is a second-grade teacher in Cedar Lake, Indiana. Every year she takes a personal day from school to attend Opening Day at Wrigley Field. "Baseball is so much more than a game," revealed Betty. "We use it at our school all the time to encourage learning." Before I left Betty she gave me a list of books I should read about the Cubs. I told her I had two of the three she recommended. Two weeks later a package arrived at the L.A. Times from Betty containing the one book I didn't own, and a kind note: "It was nice meeting you to talk about baseball and the Cubs. Wishing you luck on your journey."

I would make dozens of trips back to Wrigley Field in the years to come, and I never became jaded to the wonder of it all. Like the euphoric Cubs fans returning to the ballpark on Opening Day, I, too, was addicted to this drama of devotion that had become woven into the fabric of my life. Over the years hope would make the story grow, along with the desire to win the gamble. Even though it seems there's something about baseball that's destined to break your heart, the real fans keep coming back.

OPENING DAY DOES HOLD A MAGIC NOT OFFERED ON ANY OTHER DAY OF THE YEAR.

Cheryl Hanson and Dr. Robert Hickerson are part of a group of Cubs fans from Galesburg, Illinois, who share the tradition of passing a bottle of Drambuie to toast the Cubs season with good fortune before the Opening Day game. The Drambuie label is "A link with the '45," which Cubs fans liken to mean 1945, or the team's last World Series appearance.

The cold winds blowing in off Lake Michigan encourage these Cubs fans to be resourceful in their choice of outerwear protection from the harsh elements of an early spring day in Chicago.

Legendary "Mr Cub," Ernie Banks throws out the first pitch to begin play on Opening Day.

Cubs fans cheer when Ryne Sandberg crosses home plate with another Cubs run. This Opening Day ends with applause as the traditional white flag bearing a blue W is hoisted above Wrigley Field to send the message that today the "Cubs Win!"

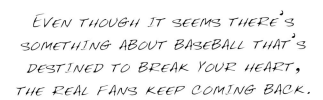

Even though it seems there's something about baseball that's destined to break your heart, the real fans keep coming back.

CHAPTER 10

A Summer Serenade

While there are so many ways to define Chicago, returning to Wrigley Field on a midsummer day with the ballpark filled to its rafters in a cachet of color and a warm breeze floating toward Lake Michigan is at the top of any baseball fan's list of "must-dos" in the Windy City.

Considered a cathedral of baseball, Wrigley Field is as much of an attraction as the Cubs themselves, and the stadium draws fans whether the team is winning or not. But Wrigley Field deserves to be admired, as it proves that character reaches its finest expression when we look beyond the patina of time and recognize the value and purpose of an extensive life span.

Even visiting ballplayers arrive at Wrigley Field with eyes wide in awe as they noticeably pause to survey this shrine to the game before stepping onto its emerald green grass. They realize that it is one of the only venues left in baseball where the game can still be experienced as it was nearly a century ago. From foul pole to foul pole, Wrigley Field's form follows function without grand embellishments and offers a refreshingly old-fashioned environment where the fans are close to the players on the field. Bringing forward the pleasure of the past into the present, there is a romantic allure to the atmosphere that transcends nostalgia and evokes the very essence of baseball.

Built in 1914, long before freeways existed, Wrigley Field stands in a neighborhood where it is best reached by train, bus, or foot. The Friendly Confines, as it is affectionately also known, does not offer much in the way of parking. Considered a "cozy" ballpark, it measures 355 feet to left, 353 to right, 400 to center, and 495 to a rooftop

The "friendly confines" of Wrigley Field display a panoramic view of the Chicago skyline on a perfect summer day during a contest against the arch rival St. Louis Cardinals. A visit to this classic ballpark for a Cubs game is a must on every baseball fan's list.

on a house across Sheffield Avenue. The division standing flags, as well as flags flying off the foul poles honoring retired numbers from famous Cubs, have a dual purpose of showing which way the wind blows. After a game a blue W on a white background flies for a win, and a white L on a blue background flies for a loss. There are also white and blue lights to signify a win or loss to train travelers passing by Wrigley Field at night.

Yet, for all the flags that fly at Wrigley there is one missing—the one that dates a World Series Championship. It seems unfitting that this sanctuary of baseball, and one of the last keepers of the game's fading traditions, should not have such a crowning glory. It's like waiting for a kiss, I thought as I arrived at Wrigley Field bright and early one morning to photograph the ground crew's daily routine of preparing the stadium for game day.

"You do this every day?" I asked groundskeeper Rick Fuhs as he made his way toward the outfield with ladder and gardening shears in hand. He was about to clip and clean the famous ivy covering the brick walls of Wrigley Field. He explained that the ivy is manicured before every game to keep it trim, and because "you never know what you might find hiding in here." With that said, Rick reached into the ivy where it met the warning track of center field and pulled out a baseball smudged with dirt. "See what I mean; this was probably a ground-rule double right here," he noted, offering me the baseball with the comment that the ballpark has a number of unique characteristics that sometimes can play into the outcome of a game.

After spending the morning with Fuhs and his crew, I realized that no one knows Wrigley Field better than these caretakers. They are like a movie star's wardrobe crew, applying the make-up and renewing the accessories that refresh the ballpark's spirit each day. As Fuhs tidied the ivy another member of the crew prepared the manual scoreboard to represent the major league games

scheduled for the day. Soon after, the game flags were organized and raised to fly above the scoreboard and the marquis. Several hours remained before the game, but it was time for the field to be readied for batting practice as the ballplayers began to stretch and sprint their way from the clubhouse. Anxious reporters followed in their wake, needing to get in an interview or two before the pre-game practice swung into high gear. Music began to play through loudspeakers soon to be accompanied by a joyous chorus of Cubs fans arriving early to take in Wrigley Field's perpetual serenade.

"Yes, we do this every day," answered Fuhs. "But somehow it always seems brand-new."

BRINGING FORWARD THE PLEASURE OF THE PAST INTO THE PRESENT, THERE IS A ROMANTIC ALLURE TO THE ATMOSPHERE THAT TRANSCENDS NOSTALGIA.

Wrigley Field's grounds crew arrives early in the morning on game days to get the stadium renewed for another full house of enthusiastic Cubs fans. Head grounds keeper Rick Fuhs manicures the famous ivy-coat on the ballpark's brick outfield wall.

Early in the morning a grounds crew member prepares the hand-operated scoreboard with the schedule of major league games on tap for the day. Later, an astonished young Cubs fan watches members of the grounds crew with lunches in hand climb a ladder leading inside the scoreboard of Wrigley Field about an hour before game time. The landmark scoreboard offers open spaces from which the grounds crew members peek out and keep an eye on the game. (Right)

CHARACTER REACHES
ITS FINEST EXPRESSION
WHEN WE LOOK BEYOND
THE PATINA OF TIME AND
RECOGNIZE THE VALUE
AND PURPOSE OF AN
EXTENSIVE LIFESPAN.

CHAPTER 11

Rooftops & Bleachers

Creating a picturesque panorama unequaled in any other major league baseball stadium, Wrigley Field's rooftop and bleacher seats unfurl with an enticing invitation as unique worlds unto themselves where fraternizing is the essence of the experience. A visit to either colorful outpost is a social gathering where no one is a stranger, and everyone assumes you must know someone.

Yet, there was a time when the rooftop experience was not at all expensive or exclusive. In fact, the Wrigley rooftops, which actually predate the ballpark, began as a casual gathering place for neighborhood fans watching the ballgames from atop the brownstones along Sheffield and Waveland Avenues. Meanwhile, the Cubs organization quietly tolerated the "freebie" perches, realizing that the rooftops were part of the enchanting recipe making up the increasingly popular old-time flavor of Wrigley Field.

Then, as Cubs fans say, too much of good thing happened when the rooftop owners began building their own little bleacher sections and charging admission. The inside of the buildings were remodeled as baseball wonderlands complete with air-conditioned lounges offering full bar and grill, giant flat-screen televisions, and surround-sound speakers. Eventually the Cubs organization, the rooftop owners, and the City of Chicago agreed to make the rooftops a legitimate, revenue-sharing extension of Wrigley Field.

Watching a Cubs game from these rooftops is truly like arriving at a balcony over baseball. An unobstructed 360-degree view takes in all of the ballpark, the full skyline of Chicago, and the surrounding neighborhood. Though the rooftop crowd is a good distance from home plate, they readily connect with the energy of the bleacher crowd.

As is true in any part of Wrigley Field, the spirit of the rooftops has as much to do with being a part of the action as it does with following the action. And nowhere is this spirit more evident than in the bleachers. From my very first visit to the bleachers, and every time since, a wonderful feeling of belonging wrapped itself around me like a welcome embrace.

Wrigley Field's rooftops and bleachers are well known features of the ballpark where Cubs fans enjoy a unique atmosphere and a special camaraderie. A "secret code" displayed by one of the rooftops (left) allegedly states "Let's Go Cubs," in Latin and respectively identifies the number of years since the last division title, league title, and World Series title.

The panoramic view from Wrigley Field's rooftops, separated from the ballpark's bleachers by Sheffield and Waveland Avenues. More than a dozen rooftops surrounding Wrigley Field provide their own bleacher sections, augmented with mounted TV sets and speakers for a close-up view of the game. Inside the buildings offer a private club atmosphere complete with air-conditioned lounges, big screen TVs, and food and beverage menus.

"It's a beautiful day," Carmella Hartigan tells me, as if I hadn't noticed. Seated on the end of the second row from the top in the midsection of the left-field bleachers, Carmella surveyed me without a question, tipped her head back to sniff the air, squinted into the sunshine with a dramatic pause, and then proclaimed, "I think the Cubs are going to win today." Her clear blue eyes twinkled with this delightful thought as she waited for me to agree. "Oh, I bet you say that every day," I responded, deciding to tease her, and asked her if she had said yesterday that the Cubs would win (because they had lost.) Quickly rising to my challenge Carmella retorted, "Oh, so what am I going to do if they lose today...cry?"

At that, Carmella and I shared the first of many good laughs to come. And within moments I learned that I just encountered the "Grand Dame" of Wrigley Field.

Always in the same seat, often wearing the same pink Cubs hat sporting a pin stating "Without the storm, there could be no rainbow," and often wielding tickets dated from a game passed, Carmella Hartigan immediately struck me as beautiful as her life is long—92 years long, in fact, when we first met. Usually an early arriver to the bleachers on game days, Carmella simply takes her seat and suddenly the world comes to her.

The first day I met Carmella she wore a Cubs T-shirt with "1908" proudly displayed across the front. She tells me that she was six-years-old when the Cubs won the World Series in '08, but she doesn't remember it because she was born in Italy and emigrated to the United States as a teenager. She arrived in Chicago in 1916, the same year the Cubs began play at Wrigley Field. Carmella is one of the few Cubs fans on earth who can even say they were alive when the Cubs last won the World Series.

I soon learned that everyone in the bleachers wants to know everything about everyone, and besides that there is a specific cast of characters who bring a regular act to this show within the show.

Maggie Lawrence began coming to Wrigley Field as a six-year-old in 1963. "I grew up in this neighborhood," she said, "and summertime to me was waking up from my afternoon nap to the sound of Harry Caray's voice singing 'Take Me Out to the Ball-game.' I really miss that...and the cookouts drifting smoke into my bedroom," she joked.

Maggie's remarks caused me to drift myself, back to my own memories of loving the Cubs as a young girl. Summer days seemed endless then, and rooting for the Cubs was a way of passing the time. Following the Cubs became my personal survival tactic, a positive diversion to less gainful alternatives and a distraction to the inevitable boredom of growing up.

The love affair continued from childhood, through adolescence, and into my adult life. Through all the changes that life brought forward, the Cubs and I stayed together—and sometimes it seemed they were the only part of life remaining constant. The Cubs were always something to look forward to no matter whether they won or lost.

Suddenly my daydream was pierced by the shrill reality of a loud scream. That's Ronnie "Woo-Woo" Wickers, the fans explained to me. He's usually heard ahead of being seen with his famous "Cubs-Woo" battle cry. Most often showing up in a full-fledged Cubs uniform, one day Ronnie arrived doing the hula hoop in a gorilla outfit.

Keeping track of the bleacher fans' daily antics is a labor of love for regular Stephanie Leathers, who circulates "The Bleacher Banter," a monthly newsletter detailing the trials and tribulations of the Cubs through the musings of the bleacher crowd.

"We're fans, and we want the Cubs to win, but if they don't win it's the same," she said and pointed out that the ending of her statement is how the bleacher fans change one lyric when singing "Take Me Out to the Ballgame." I thought back to my car ride with Charles O'Donnell to the Cubs Convention and his theory that the more things change with the Cubs, the more they stay the same. I realized that from season to season, the players come and go, but these Cubs fans are here for the duration of the drama… come what may…and as long as they are here, there will always be more to come.

Clifton Koehler of Braidwood, Illinois, brings a large fishing net along for his visit to friends who live at one of the brownstones facing Wrigley Field along Waveland Avenue (left). While Koehler hopes to snag a Cubs homerun ball, other Cubs fans enjoy watching the game and the street crowd below from the open windows of the buildings.

THE SPIRIT OF THE ROOFTOPS HAS AS MUCH TO DO WITH BEING A PART OF THE ACTION AS IT DOES WITH FOLLOWING THE ACTION.

Wrigley Field's outfield bleacher sections are famous for inciting a fun, party-like atmosphere whether attracting Cubs fans to sneak away from the office early still wearing their white shirts and ties (right), or to paint letters on their bare chests to spell out a common devotion: C-U-B-S. This foursome bearing the message includes, from left: Sam Morrison, Mike Tallon, Nick Thacker, and Philip Brown, all from Lexington, Illinois.

From season to season, the players come and go, but these Cubs fans are here for the duration of the drama... come what may.

"Oh, so what am I going to do if they lose today... cry?"

Carmella Hartigan was a mainstay in the Wrigley Field bleachers until passing away in late 2002 just shy of her 101st birthday. Considered the "Grand Dame of Wrigley Field," Hartigan wore a pin on her signature pink Cubs hat stating: "Without the storm, there could be no rainbow." Always found seated in the same row of the left field bleachers, Cubs fans enjoyed visiting with Hartigan during games, and often offered her a ride home afterward, shown here as the "Bleacher Preacher" Jerry Pritiken bids Hartigan farewell at her doorstep.

Stephanie Leathers is not only well known to Wrigley Field's bleacher crowd, but she knows all about each one of them. As a "labor of love," Leathers produces a newsletter called *The Bleacher Banter* and distributes it mostly by mail to Cubs fans with inquiring minds. Away from the ballpark she devotes the majority of her spare time to producing the newsletter at her Wrigleyville home.

"We're fans, and we want the Cubs to win, but if they don't win it's the same."

Arriving at the game Leathers readily hands out copies of *The Bleacher Banter* to her inside circle of "bleacher bum" friends at Wrigley Field. The monthly chronicle is full of news and entertaining commentary about bleacher fans, Cubs players and the fate of the current season.

After the game the bleacher crowd takes their fun along to the sports bars around the ballpark where good times can continue to roll on into the night. Bleacher buddies and fellow attorneys Tom Tonnesen of Cedarburg, Wisconsin and Fred Speck of Chicago (above) talk over prospects on the Cubs season at a Wrigleyville beer garden while wearing their signature license plates personalized with Cubs phrases.

CHAPTER 12

Wrigleyville

Nothing short of sheer magic and madness runs through the streets of Clark, Addison, Sheffield, and Waveland—the city block that hosts an ongoing baseball carnival in the midst of a neighborhood. Wrigleyville can provide so much entertainment of its own that some baseball fans forget there's a baseball game happening inside the stadium.

Beginning at the corner of Clark and Addison, where the Wrigley Field marquis flashes its "Welcome Cubs Fans" signature, a walk around the stadium quickly weaves any foot traveler into a colorful cocoon of activity, interaction, and shared affections. Dance to the cacophony produced by street musicians, stop off at the corner of Waveland and Kenmore where the territorial "ballhawks" prowl the pavement to snag the next homer clearing the outfield wall, and take a water break at the infamous Wrigleyville fire station where a street hydrant near the corner of Waveland and Seminary flows "magic water" said to bring the Cubs luck on game days.

My visits to Wrigley Field would always begin and end with this trip around the bases of Wrigleyville, and sometimes I was the Cubs fan forgetting that there was a baseball game going on inside the stadium. Often I would leave with the game hanging in the balance, venture out into the streets for a break, and fail to return. Sometimes I'd run into an actual Wrigleyville resident, such as Beth Kelly whose home along Kenmore has stood for 100 years. "Longer than the ballpark," she told me while taking a break from reading a novel and sunbathing in the front yard—a well-spotted location that

The neighborhood streets surrounding Wrigley Field are affectionately known as "Wrigleyville," and add up to an intoxicating recipe of magic and madness. Chicago police on horseback add to the atmosphere with a generally casual patrol, while a party atmosphere takes over on game days and anything goes, including groom Corey Martin and his brother and best man, Dennis, on their way to Martin's wedding reception as they pass by Cubs fans along Addison Avenue.

The Wrigleyville neighborhood begins another day quietly in the morning as a barkeep raises the shades on the Cubby Bear Saloon, located on the corner of Clark and Addison Streets across from Wrigley Field's marquis corner.

allows her to also keep track of the Wrigley Field scoreboard during the game. "People from all over say that if you haven't seen a ballgame here then you haven't seen one," she remarked. "But I've grown up in this house, and for me the Cubs are just a part of life, a part of my environment. When they're playing, though, I do always check to see if they're winning or losing," she concluded, with another quick glance up at the scoreboard.

"What's really nice is that when all the buses leave, and all the people are gone, we're still here," said ballhawk Dave Davison who lives in an apartment building right at the corner of Waveland and Kenmore. Davison invites other ballhawk regulars, such as Johnny Rosenstein, Ken Vangeloff, and Joe Flores inside his own version of "Cubdom," where hundreds of baseballs snared on the streets line the walls of his apartment. Davison shared that his total collection approaches a couple thousand, but he doesn't have the room to display them all. More than happy to spend the hours of the ballgame outside the stadium, Davison and the ballhawks are a legendary part of the Cubs atmosphere, showing up well before batting practice and holding down their corner of Wrigleyville through the chaotic hoopla that breaks out in the streets after the game's final inning.

"This is really nice," noted Isabel Trumbull, whom I found visiting with the "hawks" one Sunday afternoon. "I'm ready to grab a mitt and come out here more often, even though I haven't caught a baseball in 20 years. But I do live just six blocks away. We can actually see the games from our rooftop."

Accompanied by her four-month-old daughter napping in a stroller, Isabel explained that she and her husband, Bill, had no plans for the day, and while taking a leisurely walk they were drawn to the sound of cheering at the ballpark. Bill had just taken the two older kids to visit the Wrigleyville fire station

The bygone Yum-Yum Diner, located for decades near the ballpark's administrative parking lot, was a respite for ushers and ballplayers to drop in for breakfast or a doughnut and cup of coffee.

down the street, and she opted to sit with the ballhawks and watch the scoreboard a while. Suddenly Bill was rushing back toward Isabel flushed with excitement and waving something in his hand. "The firefighters just gave me three tickets to the game," he told her, wearing a huge smile, "because it's Father's Day!" Isabel waved him on saying, "The three of you go ahead and enjoy. I'm just fine to stay right here." Isabel moved the stroller to a shady spot as one of the ballhawks offered her his lawn chair. She settled into the chair with a sigh. "Ah, this really is so nice," she said again, this time to no one in particular.

"I can see clearly now that the Cubs have won," crooned guitarist Joe Ellison to streams of Cubs fans departing for the Addison train station after the game has ended. "I can see all obstacles in my way," he continued with the lyrics from an oldie-but-goodie. People could not help but stop and join Ellison in his musical jaunt. They smiled, laughed, sang, and danced—and I began to think that if somehow you could count all of this happiness that happens in the streets of Wrigleyville, you would see that the Cubs are not baseball's "Loveable Losers," but they are in fact the game's "Loveable Winners." Perhaps one of the few "winners" left in professional sports today. Because a baseball game at Wrigley Field, win or lose, is an absolute celebration of life—in victory, in failure, and always in good spirit. Critics may call it a giant baseball block party... but damn, it's fun.

The Wrigleyville Fire Station, located along Waveland Avenue across from the stadium's Gate K, adds to the charm of the neighborhood by serving a dual purpose of welcoming Cubs fans dropping in for a visit around the game, while operating as a real fire station.

As Engine 78 gets called out on a fire it passes by a cheering crowd of ballhawks hanging
out in lawn chairs along the corner of Waveland and Kenmore.

"PEOPLE FROM ALL OVER SAY THAT IF YOU HAVEN'T SEEN A BASEBALL GAME HERE THEN YOU HAVEN'T SEEN ONE."

A fire hydrant outside the Wrigleyville Fire Station is kept running as a fountain, and Cubs fans enjoy the tradition of taking a sip of the "magic water" to bring good luck to the team.

The second floor of the station provides a good view for off-duty fire fighters to catch a glimpse of left field and a piece of the game action.

Wrigleyville ballhawk and resident Dave Davison proudly displays a portion of his massive collection of baseballs, (in the thousands), along the walls of his brownstone apartment on the corner of Waveland and Kenmore. Davison's apartment building is opposite the corner where he and his ballhawk buddies gather during Cubs games and pick their times to work the street in anticipation of a homerun coming over the wall.

A BASEBALL GAME AT WRIGLEY
FIELD, WIN OR LOSE, IS AN
ABSOLUTE CELEBRATION OF LIFE—
IN VICTORY, IN FAILURE AND
ALWAYS IN GOOD SPIRIT.

Roving street musicians begin warming up their saxophones and bongos toward the late innings of the games at Wrigley Field. If the Cubs are winning the tempo increases even more dramatically and the Cubs fans spill onto the street with song and dance. Yet, parking anywhere along the streets surrounding the ballpark could render a broken windshield when a homerun clears the wall. The owner of this Dodge Talon, who parked along Sheffield Avenue, would've been better off taking the train to Wrigley Field, where parking a car can be an issue.

CHAPTER 13

Holy Cow!

"Ah, you can't beat fun at the old ballpark," the legendary Cubs broadcaster Harry Caray would say at least once during a game. And, like his adoring Cubs fans, Harry was a part of the fun—so much so that his on-air banter often upstaged the game. Yet, he spoke a simple language that translated into a dialogue understood by everyone—the unconditional love of baseball. And he always had fun with a game, whether it was exciting or dull, a win or a loss, or even a three-hour rain delay. Among his litany of well-known expressions, "Holy Cow!" and "Cubs Win!" remain eternal exclamation points on the end of every Cubs home run or victory.

Harry once said, "You can't buy fun. No millions can buy fun. Fun comes from the heart—and it's free." He transformed the seventh-inning stretch into a ritual at Wrigley Field with his sing-along renditions of "Take Me Out to the Ballgame," with the crowd. "All right... Lemme hear ya," he would prompt the crowd, lead them off-key, and then inspire a deafening roar in response to his concluding line, "All right... Now let's get some runs!" He kept a giant fishing net handy in the booth and, when not hooking foul balls with it, he offered it to fans as a depository of items they wanted him to autograph. He played games with ballplayers' names, often mispronouncing the complicated ones and spelling the simple ones backward to make them more interesting. And he would propose a toast to almost anything, while taking up the better part of a half-inning by acknowledging Cubs fans' birthdays, wedding anniversaries, and newborn announcements.

His schmaltzy, zany, conversational style of broadcasting never went out of style, but rather it crossed generations and time zones as a symbol of the Cubs' massive appeal, and as the very spirit of the game. While his voice reached 8 million at a time, it seemed as though he was one-on-one with each fan. His broadcasting was so beloved that when he made his three-inning switch from television to radio during games some fans muted the TV and replaced it with Harry's voice on the radio.

St. Louis was the first leg of Harry's journey to the broadcast wing of the Baseball Hall of Fame, and he was a fixture at Busch stadium for 25 years. Yet, Chicago would become Harry's definition, the place where he transcended baseball to become a household name in America, reaching a level of fame he

An icon at Wrigley Field for 16 seasons, Hall of Fame broadcaster Harry Caray was famously chauffeured to the ballpark, and then whisked away by golf cart to the broadcast booth on the upper level. But, once the ticket gates opened, he wasted no time making his way to the field to meander among the fans, the media and the ballplayers. Here Caray shares a laugh through his headset with WGN-TV producer Arnie Harris, his invisible and silent partner in the creation of fun and engaging television broadcasts.

never imagined. After announcing 11 seasons for the cross-town White Sox, Harry arrived at Wrigley Field in 1982 where he put his signature on the game for the next 16 years. He represented the fans of baseball in a way no one would dare to emulate. His presence in the broadcast booth became a consistency, and like the uniform and ballpark, he was something that didn't change from season to season. Beyond all this, his delightful delivery of Cubs ballgames is credited with sending the team's popularity to unprecedented heights during his tenure.

Yet, credit also goes to Harry's platform, a cable superstation that reached millions of baseball fans nationwide and broadcast an unprecedented number of Cubs games each season. Generations of young Chicagoans listened to Harry and the Cubs on TV after school, while stay-at-home moms (and dads) saved up the ironing for the ballgames. Even San Diego citizens voted to have a cable channel piping them Dodgers games replaced by WGN-TV and the Chicago Cubs.

During the bottom of the seventh inning Harry Caray turned the broadcast booth into a theater when he would sing "Take Me Out To The Ballgame," with the Cubs fans and often invite celebrity guests to join him. Here, Illinois native Hillary Rodham Clinton joins Caray on an Opening Day when Clinton threw out the first pitch as First Lady of the United States.

Credit also goes to Harry's supporting cast. His longtime partner in the booth and a former Cubs pitcher, Steve Stone was the straight man who kept the game on track. And Arnie Harris, the producer of WGN's Cubs broadcasts, was the shadow play behind Harry's diversions toward the boats on Lake Michigan, the ballhawks on the streets, or the antics in the bleachers. While the television viewers never saw Arnie, they heard Harry's part of their conversations on the air. And though he worked invisibly, behind the scenes, Arnie supported Harry's quest to bring the magic of the Cubs forward.

Former Cubs pitcher, and Cy Young Award Winner, Steve Stone was Caray's sidekick in the broadcast booth as well as a partner in a popular bar and grill in Mesa, Arizona named "Harry & Steve's." Stone's ability to keep focus on the play-by-play of the game allowed Caray the freedom to converse with abandon about whatever topic appealed to him in the moment.

This farm in southern Illinois sports the Cubs logo inside a cable dish.
The Cubs reach 45 million households nationally without primetime competition, as many of the broadcasts are afternoon games.

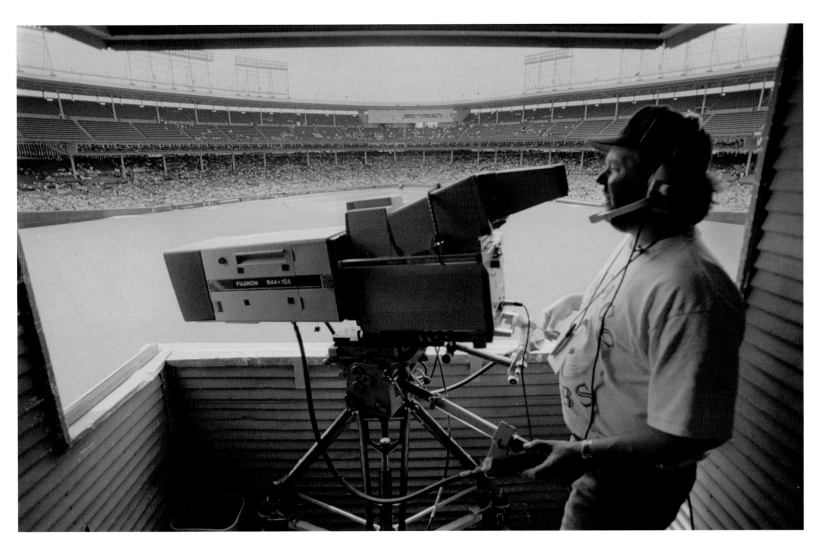

The far reach of cable superstation WGN-TV, as well as the powerful signal of WGN-Radio, often receives credit for extending the popularity of the Chicago Cubs into the hinterlands of America.

"He was our voice of summer," Chicago lamented collectively when Harry Caray passed away from a heart attack in 1998, just days before his celebrated March 1 birthday and right at the beginning of spring training. Would summer ever be the same? they wondered. In the obituaries Harry's age ranged from 79 to 83, because he was born an orphan, at large to a world that would eventually proclaim him an icon. Ironically the Cubs had planned a salute to Harry Caray in August of the '98 season, not realizing their guest of honor would be absent. Yet, they went ahead with the celebration knowing it would offer emotional closure for the millions who loved him and mourned his sudden departure. In fact, the entire 1998 season, which took the Cubs to a wild-card playoff berth, played out with so much spontaneous joy and unexpected magic that many believe Harry had a hand in it after all.

And, as fate would have it, Arnie Harris joined Harry just a few years later in what must be some other baseball heaven beyond the Friendly Confines of Wrigley Field. Arnie also passed away from a heart attack, days before the end of the 2001 season. Many imagine that the two of them were each given a standing ovation by the countless Cubs fans who also departed the planet shy of their dream to see the Cubs win the World Series. And, more than likely, Harry ends every baseball season in heaven with the same parting words he had at the conclusion of his final broadcast: "Well, folks, maybe next year will be the next year we've been waiting for forever. So long, everybody."

WGN PRODUCER ARNIE HARRIS WAS THE SHADOW PLAY BEHIND HARRY'S DIVERSIONS TOWARD THE BOATS ON LAKE MICHIGAN, THE BALLHAWKS ON THE STREETS, OR THE ANTICS IN THE BLEACHERS.

The WGN-TV broadcasts for Cubs home games are produced inside a small trailer truck, located in the administration parking lot at Wrigley Field.

Inside the WGN-TV trailer truck former broadcast producer Arnie Harris watches monitors showing various views of the game from different camera angles on the field. Harris was the visual magician behind Harry Caray's colorful commentary.

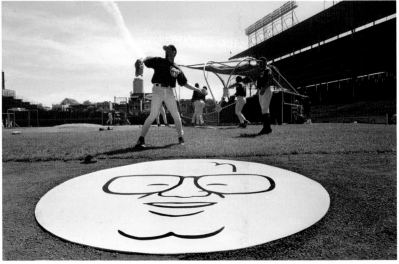

Harry Caray Day at Wrigley Field in August, 1998 was planned before his sudden death in March of that year. Yet, even without him in person, the event proved to be the perfect way to honor his career. Cubs fans wore replicas of Caray's oversized eyeglasses, and the broadcast booth remained empty that day but for a caricature of the legend.

Sports announcer Chip Caray, who succeeded his grandfather in the Cubs broadcast booth, smiles at the outpouring of love and honor displayed on Harry Caray Day at Wrigley Field.

Following the '98 season, the Cubs erected a statue of Caray at Wrigley Field near the corner of Clark and Addison Streets where Cubs fans continue to pay homage to a man they will always consider a Chicago legend.

"HE WAS OUR VOICE OF SUMMER..."

Cubs fans bid Harry Caray farewell in his own words, "So Long Everybody," which was
his final statement at the end of every Cubs game he broadcast during his 16 seasons on
the North Side of Chicago. Meanwhile bleacher fans add their own touch to the good-bye:
"We love you and miss you Harry."

CHAPTER 14

Let There Be Lights

Joe Guzman stepped off the El at the Addison Station to switch trains for his ride home after work. Dressed in a white shirt, tie, and dress slacks he carried the newspaper in hand. Brightness caught his eye like a beacon in the near distance. "Ah…the lights are on at Wrigley Field," he said out loud, "so the Cubs are playing tonight. I wish I could go." He opened the paper to find out who are the opposing pitchers and looked back longingly toward the ballpark. Moments later his train home arrived impatiently, and he quickly shared a thought with me before being whisked away into the descending dusk: "The night games are special, not too many of them…. I'm sure you'll have a great time."

His parting remark summed up the evening. Night games at Wrigley Field have a magnetic allure. Because they are staged in limited quantity, Cubs fans consider them a "special event." Generally sold out, the lively atmosphere of the night games extends into the bleachers, over the rooftops, and onto the streets of Wrigleyville with a unique intensity. After all, for many citizens of Chicago who have to maintain a nine-to-five work regimen, night games might be their only option for seeing baseball. Even if tickets are not available, the nearby sports bars are the next best place to be in Chicago on a night when the lights are on at Wrigley Field.

A longstanding distinction of the Chicago Cubs and their home ballpark was the resistance of installing lights on its rooftop. Not until August 8, 1988, a date chosen by the Cubs as easy to remember (8-8-88), did lights shine at Wrigley Field. The game that night against the Philadelphia Phillies was rained out after three and a half innings, yet it was highly entertaining nonetheless when Cubs players spontaneously ran and slid across the waterlogged infield tarp determined to anoint the evening with something memorable. The players were reprimanded and fined for their fanciful rain dance, but they went on to beat the New York Mets the next night, rendering August 9, 1988, as the Cubs' first official home night game of the 20th century.

Lights did make an appearance at Wrigley Field, however, during the off-season of 1941, as owner P.K. Wrigley ordered them to be installed for the next year. However, the bombing of Pearl

The Chicago Cubs played baseball exclusively in the daytime at Wrigley Field for 74 seasons until the Cubs organization lobbied with the local neighborhood as well as the city of Chicago for the allowance of a limited number of night games beginning August 8, 1988. Though the first game was rained out, the night games resumed, proving to be a welcome change from the heavy daytime schedule for both Cubs players and fans.

Waiting at the Addison station for the next train to take him home after a long day at the office, Cubs fan Joe Guzman notices that the lights are on at Wrigley Field. While expressing his wish that he could go to the game, Guzman checks the newspaper to see who'll be pitching for the Cubs.

Harbor changed his mind and he donated the lights to the war effort instead. After the war Wrigley changed his mind again and stated he would never install lights at the ballpark, citing a social agreement with the neighborhood as well as baseball's destiny to remain a game played only in the sunshine.

The Tribune Company, as owner of the Cubs beginning in 1981, finally won the battle when Major League Baseball pushed the Cubs to install lights or be forced to host any post-season games elsewhere, proffering enemy territories such as Busch Stadium in St. Louis or Comiskey Park on Chicago's South Side belonging to the rival White Sox as alternatives.

Determined to avert the unimaginable occurrence of Wrigley Field not being able to host its own playoff games, the Tribune Company and the Cubs organization had to volley with the City of Chicago to overturn an ordinance in association with the Lake View neighborhood that denied night games at the ballpark. A compromise was reached in early 1988 that allowed the Cubs to install lights, but they had to agree to a "limited" schedule of night games per season.

Attending night games at Wrigley Field is one of those things, Cubs fans say, that's special because "there's not too many of them." Though the sunshine and caressing breezes of a warm summer afternoon in Chicago remain the team's beloved signature, Cubs fans also say that too much of a good thing isn't always good…so bring on the night, and let there be light!

Wrigleyville comes alive with a little night music and the ballhawks chasing homeruns down Waveland Avenue.

The ballhawk crowd gathers for a casual block party at the corner of Waveland and Kenmore during a night game at Wrigley Field.

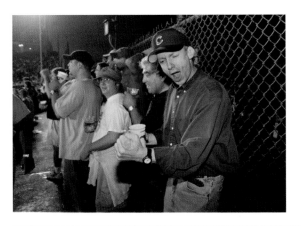

Attending night games at Wrigley Field is one of those things, Cubs fans say, that's special because there's not too many of them.

The bleacher section is standing room only as the popularity of the night games, limited to about 30 per season, attracts a large audience. Yet, the games stretch on beyond the bedtime of bleacher fan Carmella Hartigan who departs the game early to pick up a ride from a bicycle caddy and waves a good night to her bleacher friends.

CHAPTER 15

Border Battles

Interleague play prompted some Cubs fans to wear buttons saying, "JUST DON'T GO," to Comiskey Park while others embraced the chance to infiltrate enemy territory.

Though the degrees of separation can at times be slight, there is a great divide between the Cubs and their regional opponents: the Chicago White Sox, the St. Louis Cardinals, and the Milwaukee Brewers.

For most of the 20th century, any real conclusion between the Cubs and their rivals was limited to contests between the National League's Cubs and Cardinals, as the American League's White Sox and Brewers would not see Wrigley Field short of a postseason World Series matchup. Not until 1997, with the introduction of interleague play, would subjective debates go to the baseball diamond in a flurry of excitement and controversy as baseball rivals between the two leagues squared off face-to-face.

Many baseball traditionalists were clearly set against interleague play, but others embraced it as a way to enable fans to see the stars from both leagues. White Sox fans saw it as a way to taunt the Cubs fans by erecting a sign near Wrigley Field that stated: "MAJOR LEAGUE BASEBALL IS 10 MILES SOUTH." And Cubs fans called for a joint protest by wearing buttons saying: "CUBS AND SOX FANS UNITE. JUST DON'T GO."

Despite the mixed emotions, excitement was alive in Chicago the first week of interleague play during the '97 season that invited Milwaukee's "Brew-Crew" to Wrigley Field and then transported the Cubs below Madison Street to Comiskey Park. Yet, anxiety hung in the air. Which way would it go? As detailed in the media notes I picked up in the Cubs press room before the first interleague game: "Friday, June 13th, Cubs vs. Brewers, Wrigley Field. Weather: It's Chicago. You Guess."

Cubs fans had ambiguous feelings toward traveling to the South Side of Chicago for the beginning of interleague play during the 1997 season which squared off the Cubs against their American League counterparts, the rival White Sox.

THE CUBS AND WHITE SOX IS A POWERFUL RIVALRY THAT HOLDS CHICAGO BRAGGING RIGHTS SWINGING IN THE BALANCE.

The interleague games between the Cubs and the White Sox are popular, and provide for some fun bantering between fans. Here, Cubs fans (from left) Sherry Mott, Pam Mott and Kris Borsodi from northern Indiana attempt to bring a piece of Wrigley Field into Comiskey Park as "bricks 'n ivy" banners. But when turned away at the ticket gate, they return the placards to their car with good humor.

Cubs fans (from left) Rachel Lanigan, Rebecca Sambles and Brooke Hornrich from northern Indiana have no problem showing their team colors during the inaugural Cubs vs. White Sox interleague series at Comiskey Park.

Mark Loretta, Milwaukee's second baseman, showed up early for batting practice at Wrigley Field saying that he and his teammates couldn't wait for this day. "This is such a treat, especially for guys who have spent their entire careers in the American League," he said while taking in a 360-degree look around the Friendly Confines.

And the Brewers fans showed up too, making the 80-mile trek down I-94 between Milwaukee and Chicago. In fact, a home run hit into the bleachers during the first inning of the game was thrown back onto the field, as is the Cubs fans' tradition with homers hit by the opposition. But this ball was hit by a Cubs player and thrown back by a Brewers fan! Cubs fans considered the imitation a true form of flattery and described the nature of the rivalry between them and their northern Great Lakes neighbor to be "fun and friendly." As Cubs coach Billy Williams noted, "We play the game for the fans, and if they have fun with the interleague contests, then it's a good thing."

The Cubs and White Sox (also known as the "Scrubs" and the "Sux," respectively, by their opposing intercity fan base) is a powerful rivalry that holds Chicago bragging rights swinging in the balance. The teams met in the World Series of 1906 (won by the White Sox) and 90 years later, thanks to interleague play, they would meet again.

It was a historic day, honored by both teams wearing retro uniforms from the early 20th century and covered by the London Times and The New York Times. It also happened to be my birthday, June 16. And on that day, the battle of "black and blue" ended with the Cubs drawing first blood. "We came out with fire in our eyes," said Cubs first baseman Mark Grace. "I don't think anyone could have beaten us."

Cubs fans prepare for battle when the St. Louis Cardinals arrive at Wrigley Field, to take part in the intense and long-standing rivalry between the Cubs and the Cardinals. Always a sold out series, even the streets around the ball park are jammed with buses parked after dropping off scores of fans from downstate Illinois, some of them wearing "plucked" Cardinal feathers on their Cubs hats.

At Busch Stadium in St. Louis the competitive energy between Cubs and Cardinals fans is equally strong as in Chicago. Cubs fan Ronnie "Woo-Woo" Wickers runs through the stands displaying a giant Cub bear. Meanwhile, Cardinals fan Marty Prather of Springfield, Missouri gets back at the Cubs fans with a compelling message of his own. (Right)

A "real" rivalry that did not need the escort of an interleague schedule is the bitter clash of the Midwest Titans: the Cubs of Chicago versus the Cardinals of St. Louis. Known as a battle that separates towns, families, and relationships, the Cardinals influence in southern Illinois can result in a Cubs fan and a Cardinals fan sharing the same dinner table…and worse.

"We really hate the Cardinals," exclaimed Cheryl Hanson and Laura Rushing, my Cubs fan friends met initially at the convention and again at Wrigley Field passing the Drambuie on Opening Day. "But the funny thing about Galesburg is that it's truly divided between the Cubs and the Cardinals. That's the way it is down here."

By "down here," they mean downstate Illinois, where White Sox fans are not Cubs fans' nemesis, but anyone who wears red is a target of their angst. Beyond Opening Day, Cheryl and Laura's favorite time of the baseball season is when the Cubs play the Cardinals at Wrigley Field. "We take the train to Chicago, and it's just a huge party with everyone wearing either blue or red. The train and bus trips from this part of the state are a big deal for the Cubs-Cardinals games, and we all look forward to them every year."

Meanwhile, Cardinals fans cannot wait for the Cubs fans to visit them in St. Louis as they say the games "bring out the best in us…. The most fun, excitement, color, and flavor that baseball can offer." They enjoy their own version of the Mason-Dixon Line, where brother and sister, father and son, and best friends divide.

The ballplayers respect this rivalry as well, because these are games that carry great significance within the standings of the NL Central Division, where both teams compete for the top spot. Today's game is a classic seesaw battle with lots of home runs and comebacks on both sides. Ronnie Woo entertains the crowd by running through the aisles wielding a gigantic blue bear. And Cubs fan Randy Hendrix follows in Ronnie's path, pointing at the Arch visible over the roofline of Busch Stadium and telling the Cardinals fans "that is the Gateway to Chicago." He also offers to sell his Cubs hat to any Cardinals fan willing to pay out $6,000. The game, on the field and in the stands, scuffles its way through 13 innings and offers a little bit of everything except a Cubs victory.

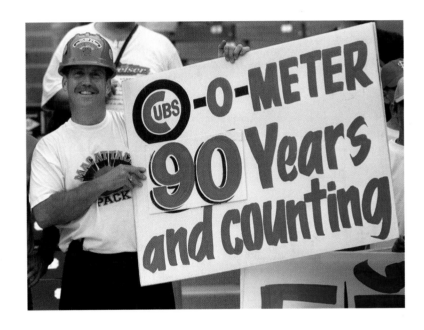

THE CUBS VS. THE CARDINALS – A BATTLE THAT SEPARATES TOWNS, FAMILIES AND RELATIONSHIPS.

Randy Wanek of Milwaukee, Wisconsin shows up at the Wrigley Field marquis wearing a Cubs cap and a Brewers jersey, saying that he grew up with the Brewers as his American League favorite, and the Cubs as his National League favorite.

Now that the Cubs and Brewers are in the same division of the National League, the "Cheeseheads" of Milwaukee descend upon Chicago wanting to win - but, they also say it remains a "friendly" rivalry between the Great Lakes neighbors, separated by only 80 miles.

CHAPTER 16

Road Trips

A phenomenon of the Chicago Cubs' popularity is their ability to achieve the highest road attendance in major league baseball, even during seasons when they have finished in last place. Many credit the extended reach of WGN broadcasts for the Cubs' transcending all others as the fair-haired boys of summer. Yet, Cubs fans come out of the woodwork all over America's hinterland, and they have never hopped the Red Line to Wrigley or pounded beers at Murphy's Bleachers. Call them the "far-flung" Cubs fans, if you will, each with his or her own unique yet familiar story as to what drew him or her into the grips of a love affair with a team known for breaking hearts. Of course, I understand them, because after all, I am one of them.

Many cite the traditions surrounding the team and the simple beauty of Wrigley Field as what compelled them to jump on a bandwagon labeled "The Loveable Losers." Meanwhile, others cite '69, '84, '89, '98, and '03 as the seasons behind the reason why they got caught up in the Cubs mystique.

But a close examination of Cubs fans' true feelings renders the critical mass. It's because the stakes are so high. The thrill is so electric. It is the tantalizing dream of arriving at what could only be imagined as one of the greatest moments in the history of sports.

The Chicago Cubs often draw the highest road attendance in the major leagues. Cubs manager Jim Riggleman is greeted by fans even in arch-rival St. Louis.

A testament to the Chicago Cubs coast-to-coast popularity, California Cubs fans show up early to begin invading Dodger Stadium with their own version of "blue," and official proclamations of their love for the Cubs.

Cubs manager Dusty Baker has some fun on the road with "Flat Stanley," a paper doll made by his son Darren for a school project where the object is to write about the different places "Flat Stanley" visits.

CUBS FANS COME OUT OF THE WOODWORK ALL
OVER AMERICA'S HINTERLAND, AND THEY HAVE
NEVER HOPPED THE RED LINE TO WRIGLEY OR
POUNDED BEERS AT MURPHY'S BLEACHERS.

**Cubs fans Jerry Russell (left)
and John Sidders of San Diego
sport fake goatees in support and
emulation of Cubs pitcher Matt
Clement during his game night at
Anaheim Stadium.**

FOR EACH AND EVERY ONE OF US THERE WAS A SPECIAL STORY, BUT A SIMILAR REASON BEHIND OUR COMMON LOVE AFFAIR WITH THE CHICAGO CUBS.

Lee Smith (above), an usher at San Diego's Petco Park, is a member of the Cubs "Die-Hard" Fan Club as a lifelong fan of the Cubs and a native of Chicago. He says he looks forward to the Cubs road trips to San Diego all year long. Celebrity Bill Murray, also an Illinois native, is shown here chatting with Cubs manager Don Baylor during batting practice at San Diego, and often shows up to root for his "Cubbies" when the team is in California.

Love for the Cubs sprouts as tall as the corn surrounding Des Moines, Iowa, the home of the Triple A farm team of the Chicago Cubs. Every so often the "Big Cubs," as the locals call them, show up to great fanfare and play an exhibition game with the "Little Cubs." The game promises to be a "no-lose" situation in this hotbed of Cubs mania, because no matter the outcome the Cubs win! But beyond that, the appearance of the major league Cubs to these die-hard followers in the midst of Iowa validates their long-term devotion. For many of them this is the first time, and may remain one of the few times, they will actually see the Chicago Cubs in person.

I can attest that absence truly does make the heart grow fonder, as I recall my first visit to Dodger Stadium to cover the Cubs for the L.A. Times. It is simply an amazement to be in real time and space with something adored at a distance for so long. It's just a difficult feeling to describe. I also recall the first time I brought my younger brother, Steve, along when the Cubs were in L.A., and as we walked onto the field where the Cubs were in the midst of their stretching exercises I heard him say under his breath: "Wow, there's the Hawk, and there's Ryno, Grace, Maddux…" Thinking maybe he could put his feelings into words I asked him: "How does it make you feel?" And he answered: "Like I'm five years old again."

As so many Cubs fan do, I passed the tradition down to the younger generation by infusing my younger brother with everything Cubs from the time he was one year old. In fact, we even made up a song that recited the Cubs lineup, and names like Ernie Banks and Billy Williams were among his first spoken words. Over the years I would buy him Cubs memorabilia and collect autographs of his favorite Cubs, hoping to assuage the pain of the unrequited love I'd cursed him with as a baby.

Sammy Sosa receives a handshake from a young San Francisco Giant fan during a Cubs road game in the Bay area.

Because of my home base in California, most of my coverage of the Cubs on the road was in Los Angeles, San Diego, San Francisco, and, thanks again to interleague play, Anaheim. And every season, no matter whether the Cubs were having one of their rare pennant runs or not, the stadiums would sell out. For me it was an opportunity to meet the far-flung Cubs fans like myself and learn that for each and every one of us there was a special story, but a similar reason behind our common love affair with the Chicago Cubs.

Some call it a curse, others consider it a commitment, but for all it is clearly a choice, and one they say remains forever once the "Cubs bug" has bitten them.

131

Cubs fans in Des Moines, Iowa, home of the Chicago Cubs Triple A
farm team, the Iowa Cubs, are thrilled to see the major league players
come to town. A fun exhibition game is played at Principal Park,
within eyeshot of the Iowa state capitol building.

CHAPTER 17

Wild Ride

It was a magic carpet that brought the Cubs into the playoffs in 1998. And for me it remains a season remembered as the most enchanting of any along my journey. Perhaps that's because it was so unexpected, in the wake of Ryne Sandberg's retirement and Harry Caray's passage to the afterworld.

But wouldn't you know it all came down to the last pitch of the last game of the regular season—a game the Cubs were not playing. It was San Francisco versus Colorado, and Neifi Perez became an unlikely hero to Cubs fans as he hit a home run in the bottom of the ninth to beat the Giants, rendering them tied at season's end with the Cubs for the right to the National League's wild-card playoff spot. From one moment to the next on a Sunday afternoon, Cubs fans went from feeling a chill in the air, seeing the leaves turning brown, and recognizing the loneliness that creeps up when your team's season ends, to feeling a sudden and unexpected euphoria of anticipating a postseason.

Suddenly, the idea of the Chicago Cubs as a team of destiny took flight, though for only the third time since their World Series defeat of 1945. The long road to the playoffs was known by Cubs fans only as "the road less traveled." It's a time in baseball when everything is magnified, because everything accomplished in the past five months doesn't matter unless you do it again now. The postseason gathers a renewed, intensified energy. And they say, "It ain't over till the Fat Lady sings."

I was stunned when I heard the final score of the Giants-Rockies game that Sunday afternoon, nearly paralyzed by the emergent reality that came forward. There was going to be a tie-breaker at Wrigley Field tomorrow, I

Cubs fans were ecstatically surprised by the spontaneous wild card tie-breaker between the Cubs and San Francisco Giants at the finish of the 1998 season. Steve Honacki of Chicago (left) alerts the Cubs of the "do or die" situation while a group of bleacher fans get into the spirit of the "wild" night by donning joker hats. Included from left are Michele and Paul Bolger, Amy Carr, Colleen Stone and Troy Anderson.

As a one game playoff to break a tie for the National League wild-card berth between the Cubs and Giants, the game would determine which team advanced into the 1998 post-season. As noted on the Wrigley Field scoreboard, it was the only game scheduled in the major leagues that day, a Monday night after the last day of the season.

Cubs fans considered it a miraculous co-incidence that the last time the Cubs were involved in a tie-breaker was in 1908 against the New York Giants. The Cubs won that game to advance to a World Series victory, which remains their last one to date. The prevailing thought ninety years later was that perhaps history would repeat with another tie-breaker victory.

No team would've beaten the Cubs that night. It was simply their destiny, and it was apparent from the first pitch to the final out.

The Chicago police contain the street crowd behind barriers at the corners of Waveland and Kenmore until a creative endeavor breaks loose toward the late innings of the wild card game. (Right)

When a group of Cubs fans launch a giant balloon bearing the likeness of Harry Caray into the night sky over Wrigley Field, the packed stadium lets out a thunderous roar, and the Cubs go on to win the game and advance to the post-season.

The surreal magic and unexpected excitement of the wild card tie-breaker lands the Cubs in Atlanta for the division series playoff.

On a plane early the next morning, I plotted out my strategy based on an early afternoon arrival in Chicago. I would take the train from O'Hare to downtown, I decided, then take the Red Line straight to Wrigley Field. No time to check into a hotel; what should I do with my luggage? I wondered. My mind went over different possibilities before arriving at a perfect solution—the Wrigleyville fire station. From the Addison train stop I ran to the fire station where the officers needed little explanation from me before agreeing to lock up my luggage for the night. Thankful to be lightened of the load, I headed back out to the streets of Wrigleyville and suddenly felt the acute presence of a surreal anticipation suspended in the atmosphere. It was a different feel from what I'd grown familiar with at the ballpark, and I decided to make a full circle around the streets to better acquaint myself with the new sensation.

Like soldiers positioned for an ensuing battle, everyone, I found, was where they should be ahead of time. The rooftop crowds were already perched on their lookouts, the ballhawks were holding down their corner with spread legs and folded arms, the bleacher bums were fully gathered and bantering beneath the scoreboard, the street musicians were entertaining arriving fans with lively tunes. And everyone I made eye contact with stared back at me with an intense awareness, as if to say, "We expected you to be here, too." It was the first time I realized that I had become a part of the story, and to them I was another one of the expected characters doing the expected thing in their world.

I must say that of all the Cubs games I've had the great fortune of witnessing firsthand, this game and this night remains an unparalleled experience. The Cubs won this game, but as Giants slugger Barry Bonds would say the next day, no team would've beaten the Cubs that night. It was simply their destiny, and it was apparent from the first pitch to the final out.

The Cubs players would remark that they also felt the presence of a force outside of themselves, as if the Cubs fans had entered the playing field that night and willed the game to victory. The players pointed toward a moment in the middle of the game when a thunderous roar was heard for no apparent reason, and they looked up to see a gigantic balloon of Harry Caray's face floating above the baseball diamond. "When I saw Harry up there in the sky," said Mark Grace, "I knew we would win the game."

It was a miraculous outcome punctuating a wild ride of a season that proved the Cubs to be nearly metaphysical. It was a night when everyone felt fulfilled by a Chicago romance that never goes away. "But be careful what you wish for…," said the Cubs fans, adding another bit to their mantra of "Wise men say only fools rush in."

From a rockin' Wrigley Field the Cubs rushed into Atlanta to a hushed stadium with 10,000 empty seats suggesting that it must be more fun to be a Cubs fan at a wild-card tie-breaker than a Braves fan at a playoff game. Known for expecting their team to make it to the World Series, the Braves fans were simply expressing that for them it wasn't near party time and that the Cubs series would be a mere blip on their Richter scale.

Meanwhile, Cubs fans who couldn't make the quick turnaround to Atlanta gleefully gathered at the sports bars around Chicago. The city was enjoying a glorious Indian summer, the Cubs were in the playoffs, and life couldn't be any better. When I heard that Dutchie Caray, widow of Harry, would be singing the seventh-inning stretch at Harry Caray's restaurant, I was excited to go and join the crowd.

The Cubs readily lost the first two games of the series in Atlanta and returned to Chicago needing to win the next game or it was curtains on the magic show of '98. Earlier that day I called a Northwest ticket agent to arrange a return flight home. I explained the Cubs would play that night and asked about flights available for the next day or the day following. "What kind of a Cubs fan are you?" the agent challenged me. "Don't you think they'll win one game at home?" We agreed to set my return to accommodate the possibility that the Cubs would win one. And as it turned out I ended up with a day off in the Windy City. I remember feeling a chill in the air, seeing the leaves turning brown, and loneliness crept up on me as I walked past Wrigley Field to take the train toward the airport. "See you next year," we said to one another.

Cubs fans gather at Chicago sports bars to watch the games on big screen televisions. At Harry Caray's Restaurant, Caray's widow Dutchie is among a crowd of Cubs fans despondently following the Cubs back-to-back losses to the Braves.

I REMEMBER FEELING A CHILL IN THE AIR,
SEEING THE LEAVES TURNING BROWN,
AND LONELINESS CREPT UP ON ME.

With the '98 division series coming back to Chicago for another "do or die" game, Cubs fans dress up the rooftops with bunting, fill the streets of Wrigleyville, and pin the hope of an entire season on the young arm of pitcher Kerry Wood. Completing a phenomenal rookie season, Wood fell short of the task of advancing the Cubs.

CHAPTER 18

Five Outs Away

The Cubs entered a Brave New World in 2003 with manager Dusty Baker determined to create a reality not focused on the past. Chanting a mind-altering mantra—"Why not us?"—Baker charged forward in his first year at the helm and delivered "Dustiny" to Wrigley Field in the final weekend of the season.

And my timing was, yet again, just right. As the last month of the season played out, it was a true roll of the dice as to whether the Cubs would win the Central Division. Teetering between miracle and disaster in the final days, they were coming down the stretch nearly deadlocked for the Central Division crown with the Houston Astros. It was unpredictable, but Cubs fans, myself included, realized that the last two days of the season would decide the outcome.

As always, I pondered my own game plan during the flight. Once again I would be touching down at O'Hare to jump the trains to Wrigley Field and arrive just as the Cubs wrapped a doubleheader. While in flight I asked the attendants if they knew the score of the Cubs games, and they did not. I would find out from someone at the airport, I decided, and immediately began scouting for an informant the moment I stepped off the plane. Quite handily I spotted a man wearing a Cubs cap, and I approached with the question. He looked at me with wide eyes and said, "Houston lost. The Cubs won the first game, and they're winning the second." "Oh my goodness," I thought in complete surprise, "I have to get there; it's about to happen!" I changed plans from taking the train to hopping in a cab.

I'll never forget that ride to Wrigley Field. With the radio blaring announcer Ron Santo's voice pitching with excitement and cracking with emotion, the cab driver and I became manic listening to the final innings of the game. As we approached Wrigley Field the Chicago police had already

Cubs fans celebrate the return of the post-season to Wrigley Field in the moments following the clinch of the National League division title in 2003. As jubilation dances through the streets of Wrigleyville, the Cubs pennant (left) flies above the bar to show the team's first place finish during the inaugural year of manager Dusty Baker's tenure.

BAKER CHARGED
FORWARD IN HIS FIRST
YEAR AT THE HELM AND
DELIVERED "DUSTINY" TO
WRIGLEY FIELD.

With the Waveland Avenue crowd enjoying the thrill of victory, and ecstatic Cubs fans posing for commemorative photos in front of Harry Caray's statue, it appears that Dusty Baker truly had a "mojo," for success. Cubs fans embraced his philosophy as some sort of intuitive magic that boldly denied past failure and asked the question: "Why Not Us?"

Finally succeeding to get past the Atlanta Braves in the division series, the Cubs advanced to the National League championship pennant series with the Florida Marlins. As the city of Chicago dresses itself in everything "Cubs" and calls for a "Fish Fry," it appeared the team was riding a wave of serendipity that was rolling its way straight to the World Series.

Determined to reverse any lingering "curses," Sam Sianas of the Billy Goat Café brings a goat to Wrigley Field for Game 6 of the pennant series. Meanwhile Cubs fans show confidence that they have a golden opportunity ahead, needing to win just one of the remaining two games with star pitchers Mark Prior and Kerry Wood ready to go.

barricaded the streets leading toward the stadium. From a distance of a quarter mile I could feel the vibrating roar of the massive crowd on hand at the ballpark, ready to explode into an ecstatic joy. "This is good right here," I told the driver, who managed to edge his way nearly to the corner of Clark and Addison. No sooner did I step onto the street than a flood of Cubs fans began pouring out of Wrigley Field in delirious celebration. The Wrigley Field marquis quickly trumpeted their news: CUBS WIN!

Once again I made my way to the fire station and said, "I'm back! May I stow my luggage once more?" The firefighters were happy to oblige, already partying in the streets with the zealous Cubs fans. Right away I spotted my bleacher friends dancing with the ballhawks along Kenmore. It amused me endlessly that they never asked me how I got there; they just expected I would somehow show up, no matter how much time had passed between visits. In fact, they acted like I lived right around the corner.

I COULD HEAR THE COLLECTIVE VOICE OF CHICAGO WHISPER UNDER ITS BREATH, "THE CUBS ARE GOING TO THE WORLD SERIES."

Cubs fans' hearts swelled with more pride than anticipated on the final day of the 2003 season. As all-time great Cubs third baseman Ron Santo's No. 10 was raised on the flagpole to accompany Banks's No. 14 and Williams's No. 26, the Chicago Cubs pennant flew above the bar that divided them from the rest of the NL Central Division. Cubs fans held up signs saying: "This season's for you, Ron Santo. A Perfect 10," and "Dusty's Mojo Worked!" Santo gave an emotional speech to the sold-out stadium and summed it up by saying that this day, dedicated to retiring his number, couldn't have been scripted any better than it turned out. "The only thing that could make it better," he told the revved up crowd, "is for the Cubs to go all the way!"

As always, the road to the playoffs would go through Atlanta. But behind a solid pitching staff and a lineup clicking on all cylinders, the Cubs quelled the Braves fans' famous war chant and buried their tomahawks. Dusty Baker had indeed guided the Cubs through the roiling wave of past failure, and it appeared they were on a forward roll. When questioned by the media for his secret to success, Dusty answered: "Sometimes you have these—what do you call them?—epiphanies in the night." Whatever the "mojo" that Cubs fans claimed Dusty Baker possessed, it was working like a charm. Now, the only thing in the way of a World Series would be the Florida Marlins. While the Cubs fans optimistically called for a "fish fry" at Wrigley Field, they also would say later, "Be careful what you wish for…" because aren't the best-told "fish stories" about the ones that got away?

With blazing fanfare the Cubs left Chicago with a split and then won two of three in Florida, bringing them back to Wrigley Field with the need to win one of the two remaining games. I could hear the collective voice of Chicago whispering under its breath: "The Cubs are going to the World Series." I made an arrangement with the Cubby Bear Saloon to photograph from their rooftop at the end of Game 6, certain the Cubs would win right away, and there would be a historic scene of celebration beneath the Wrigley Field marquis. The agreement was that I had to arrive by the eighth inning in order to be escorted to the rooftop before the streets became impassable. At the top of the eighth, with one out, I left Wrigley Field and headed for the Cubby Bear with a pounding heart and the Cubs winning 3–1.

For some unexplainable reason, the guiding spirit departed Wrigley Field right then and there with five outs to go. It would be hashed and rehashed as to what was the defining moment of the tragedy. Was it the fan reaching for the foul ball that might have been caught for an out? Was it the ball booted for an error at shortstop that might have been a double play? Was it the fact that with one game left to play the next day the Cubs could not overcome the disappointment of the fish that got away?

As the Cubs marched through Game 6 in command, the eighth inning showed them winning 3-1 with five outs to go. Expecting a victory, fans and media took places for the celebratory moment when the Cubs would clinch a World Series berth. Yet, a stunning turn-around changed the game's direction within a matter of minutes. As the Marlins scored seven runs to take the lead Cubs fans are crushed, and TV anchor Diann Burns, who is set up to go live on top of the Cubby Bear restaurant, stands frozen in confusion as to what to say to her audience of millions.

his lifelong devotion to the Cubs. He glanced toward me with tears forming in his eyes and I said to him: "Wait until next year?" He took a moment to collect himself before he replied, "Yes, that'll be true. But right now I'm here. I'm still in this year." As he spoke, a strong, cold wind kicked up and blew left to right, across the flags of Banks, Santo, and Williams, and disappeared into the night.

The train back to downtown and my hotel seemed frozen in motion. Silence was everywhere, but for the painful sound of grown men crying into their hands. I looked sadly at my cell phone, which I had programmed with my brother Steve's number. My plan was to call him from the rooftop of the Cubby Bear and let him hear the jubilant crowd below shouting "Cubs win!"

A few days following my return home my brother called me instead, and after our painful but necessary commiseration, he told me a story that returned dignity to my senses. Living in Maine as an attorney by day and a high school football coach the rest of the time, my brother Steve went to football practice the day after the Cubs' "lights out" Game 7 wearing the hat he always wears, his Chicago Cubs cap. "You wouldn't believe the look on the kids' faces," he told me, "when I walked up to them with that hat on. It was like the C turned into the Scarlet Letter. So, I asked them, 'What are you looking at?' And no one had the courage to speak. So I told them, 'Tonight your team, the Boston Red Sox, will play their Game 7 with the Yankees. And if your team loses, because that just might happen, I want every one of you to get up in the morning, like I did today, and put your damn Red Sox hat right back on again.'"

As we know, the Red Sox lost, too. And the myth of the Cubs and the Red Sox being the two cursed teams of baseball lived on for one more year—until the Red Sox avenged themselves in '04 and won the World Series. Of course, that moved into view the White Sox drought of 88 years without a World Series appearance. But they stepped out of the dubious spotlight with a World Series victory in '05. There's really only one way to look at this situation, say the Cubs fans, "Why not us?"

Game 7 the next night ended without exhale. I remember the look on the face of an old Cubs fan standing near me as he stared out at the field, empty but for the opposing players dancing their victory on Cubs turf. He seemed to be looking through the present moment and bringing forward years of time, 70 years or more, of

Although there remained another day offering the final and deciding Game 7, it seemed that the tragedy of letting Game 6 slip away erased the confidence of Cubs players and fans. The Cubs would lose the final game, curses would linger, and deeply depressed Cubs fans depart Wrigley Field to face the chill of a long, harsh winter still asking the question, "Why Not Us?"

Part Four

DECADES OF DEVOTION

THE DECADES EVOLVED THROUGHOUT THE 20TH CENTURY AS A STORIED HISTORY

A view from behind home plate off the rooftop of Wrigley Field where the Cubs bear emblem flag flies proudly above the skyline of Chicago, a place the Cubs organization has called home since 1870, and Wrigley Field since 1914.

CHAPTER 19

Great Beginnings

The early decades of the Chicago National League Baseball Club sowed the seeds of greatness and began what evolved throughout the 20th century as a storied history of one of the game's most beloved franchises.

Chicago joined the fledgling National Association of Professional Baseball in 1870 as the Chicago White Stockings, and by 1876 the team had acquired some key players, namely Adrian "Cap" Anson, who brought them to their first pennant. Anson went on to pace the White Stockings to five pennants between 1880 and 1886. He became known as "Cap" after being named captain/manager of the club in 1879.

Anson's aggressive play and prolific hitting remain legendary. It was his influence that renamed the ball club the Colts, from 1890 to 1897, as the influx of new players he signed were known as "Anson's Colts." Yet, as a manager Anson failed to win another pennant, and he was fired after the 1897 season. His departure influenced another new name for the team, the Orphans, from 1898 to 1901. Today, beyond the turn of two centuries, Anson remains the Cubs franchise record holder for runs scored (1,719), runs batted in (1,879), hits (2,995), singles (2,246), and doubles (528). Considered one of the most famous and talented ballplayers of his day, Anson ran for office and was elected sheriff of Chicago in 1907.

The Chicago ballclub awaited new leadership after Anson's retirement, and along with a new name in 1902, the Cubs began a comeback to their early success when Joe Tinker, Johnny Evers, and Frank Chance first took the field together in September of that season. Together, this infamous trio formed the nucleus of what became one of the most dominant baseball teams of all time. Along with Mordecai "Three-Finger" Brown anchoring a dominant pitching staff, Tinker, Evers, and Chance steered the Chicago Cubs to what remains their greatest success—four pennants and two World Series titles (1907 and 1908) over a five-year span (1906–1910).

Adrian "Cap" Anson, (left) was the first Chicago Cubs superstar from 1876 to 1897. Mordecai Brown (top) pitched the Cubs to a World Series championship in 1908, and Gabby Hartnett guided the Cubs to four pennants from 1929-1938.

Unfortunately, the Chicago Cubs' early glory was unknown to Wrigley Field, as the ballpark did not exist until 1914. The Cubs did not play at the venue until 1916 when William Wrigley became part investor, and then controlling owner in 1918, as Grover Cleveland Alexander pitched the team to another NL pennant. The stadium became known as Cubs Park until renamed Wrigley Field in 1926.

Between 1924 and 1928 Wrigley spearheaded extensive remodeling projects resulting in a double-decked stadium with a seating capacity nearing 40,000. This expansion allowed the Cubs to become the first major league baseball team to pass the 1 million mark in season attendance during the 1927 campaign. With marquis players such as catcher Gabby Hartnett and outfielder Hack Wilson, the Cubs were on the verge of another successful run. All told, four NL pennants concluded in four World Series defeats at Wrigley Field from 1929 to 1938.

It was during this time that Wrigley Field's most unique features were designed and constructed. Under the direction of Philip K. Wrigley, William's son, aided by the blossoming genius of a young promoter, Bill Veeck, the bleachers were added, the scoreboard was built, and many of the physical nuances, such as the outfield ivy, were implemented. Always in the forefront of marketing genius, the Cubs also brought in baseball's first organ and "Ladies Day" promotion and helped promote the All-American Girls Baseball League during the lean years of World War II.

But 1945 was a breakout year—for the country and for the Chicago Cubs. It became a year of celebration with the long war ending and the allies victorious. It was a baseball season punctuated by a World Series matchup between Chicago and their Great Lakes neighbor, Detroit. The series went seven games, and a Billy goat showed up at the gates to bring the Cubs luck. But denied entrance to Wrigley Field, the owner of the Billy goat set a curse in motion on that day that shall remain in motion until acted upon by an outside force.

CHAPTER 20

Curse of the Last Dance

"We Got Detroit's Goat," claimed the banner on the side of the goat brought by Billy Sianas to Wrigley Field during Game 4 of the 1945 World Series. A big Cubs fan, the charismatic owner of the Billy Goat Tavern was allowed to parade the goat on the field before the game. He then watched the game with his goat from the two seats he purchased for $7.20 each. All was well until fans nearby complained about the goat's offensive odor. Sianas was told, "Your goat stinks," and he was asked to leave. Denied his intention of bringing luck to the Cubs, Sianas departed scorned and immediately sent a telegram to P.K. Wrigley cursing the Cubs.

While the exact phrasing of the infamous threat is debated, the "Curse of the Billy Goat" remains a force in motion, as the Cubs have not returned to the World Series since 1945.

A visit to the Billy Goat Tavern breathes life into the superstition. Lining the walls are framed news articles penned over the decades by Chicago's well-known sports journalists, each story lending credence to the curse. Beyond this, Billy Sianas himself comes forward through the personage of his nephew Sam, who owns and operates the tavern, and continues to bring alleged "descendants" of the original Billy goat to Wrigley Field in attempts to rue the curse away.

Yet, the Billy Goat Tavern is not the only haunt in Chicago where outstanding superstitions about the Cubs fortunes are guarded. In Berwyn-Cicero, an area in the city's western suburbs still reflective of its founding bohemian ethnicity, an invitation issued from train station agent Charles O'Donnell awaited me. "Come see us at the Hourglass during the season," Charles bid after dropping me off at the Cubs Convention in January. "It's just a little hole-in-the-wall, but it's our little place to gather, and we have a good time there, complaining about the Cubs," he shared. "In fact, we say the Hourglass got it's name because we all believe that time might be running out on us old Cubs fans."

By "us old Cubs fans," I discovered, Charles was referring to a group of men, mostly retired, in the age range of 55–75, for whom the dream of seeing the Chicago Cubs win a World Series is a lifelong pursuit and a wish they exceedingly must admit is eluding them.

Sam Sianas displays the original newspaper clipping of his uncle William "Billy" Sianis getting ejected from Wrigley Field along with his goat, an incident leading to the infamous "Curse of the Billy Goat," during the 1945 World Series. Sam Sianas, who runs the Billy Goat Tavern (left) in downtown Chicago, makes random appearances with a goat at Wrigley Field in attempts to reverse the curse, and bring the Cubs good luck.

"TIME MIGHT BE RUNNING OUT
ON US OLD CUBS FANS..."

"It goes a little deeper for us here at the Hourglass, and I guess you could say it goes a little deeper here in Chicago," said Jim Downs, co-owner of the Hourglass along with his wife, Ida. "But I think it's in little taverns like this one, all over the city, where you'll find the real Cubs fans."

Charles agreed with Jim. "Here's the thing about Cubs fans," he chimed, "and I know I already told you this, but it's an expression that deserves repeating: 'The more things change, the more they stay the same.' I remember being a teenager, and I'd tell my friends I'm going to see the Cubs, and they'd complain to me about things like, the Cubs fans are all a bunch of rich people, or about how the Cubs invented Ladies Day. Now here we are, more than 50 years later, and by God we're still complaining!"

As I got acquainted with this merry band of "old Cubs fans," I began to wonder if they really wanted things to change. Listening to their stories of unrequited love and devotion to the Cubs caused me to liken their passion to a memory of the girl they never kissed, a romantic thrill of the chase. Would having it all ruin it? Are they so comfortable and accustomed to their routine and their roles that they fear anything different?

I posed the question at large, and Jim Downs took the challenge of providing an answer.

"First of all," he began, "we'll never give up, because if you give up then you don't deserve it. But we say sometimes that if they win it all, maybe some of the habit we've developed will disappear. After all, people are creatures of habit, and we really have one big habit going on here. Maybe the beauty of the whole thing is that we enjoy trying."

To demonstrate his philosophy, Jim quickly went behind the bar, reached behind the cash register, and brought out a whiskey bottle designed as a Cub bear, complete with uniform and ball cap. "I bought this bottle of whiskey in 1945," Jim said. "It was for celebrating the Cubs winning the World Series that year. As you can see, it's never been opened. But, it's right here, waiting for the day with the rest of us. So, I guess you could say, for this whiskey bottle anyway, it's finest moment is yet to arrive. And I believe we all need something to look forward to.... Don't you agree?"

Jim Downs, at right, owner of the Hourglass in Berwyn, shares a laugh with long-time friend and patron Charles O'Donnell. The tavern, located in the western suburbs of Chicago, is a hangout for a group who call themselves "old Cubs fans." Near the tavern's cash register, Downs displays a bottle of whiskey in the shape of a Chicago Cubs bear, (left top) purchased in 1945 with the intention of celebrating a Cubs World Series victory. The bottle was never opened, and it waits along with Downs and his baseball buddies for the Cubs to renew the opportunity.

CHAPTER 21

Heartbreak — '69

As I would come to learn, all Cubs fans harbor a particular season of heartbreak—also known as the year they believed the curse would reverse. Spinning forward from the disappointment of 1945, the Cubs wheel of fortune paused on destiny once again in 1969. This season was the pinnacle of a resurgence that began in the mid-1960s behind players whose names and accomplishments are forever imbedded in the tapestry of history defining the franchise: Banks, Williams, Jenkins, and Santo.

Yet, 1969 became a bittersweet memory of hope that collapsed into a crushing blow when the Cubs, who led the Eastern Division for most of the season, faltered and finished in second place, eight games behind the New York Mets. It was a loss destined to send an entire generation of Cubs fans cycling through the stages of grief for years to come. By the early 1970s this memorable Cubs team had dissolved, and its destiny of greatness would result in three Hall of Fame inductions: Ernie Banks, Billy Williams, and Ferguson Jenkins (and Cubs fans add, "Why not Ron Santo?").

I decided to root for the Cubs in '69, because I thought it a shame for these great players to remain unadorned by the World Series. After all, Ernie Banks, the famous "Mr. Cub," was just a step away from concluding a career he began in 1953. Nineteen sixty-nine saw Banks approaching 500 home runs and standing on the threshold of Cooperstown. It seemed unconscionable that a player whose contributions defined him as one of baseball's greatest ambassadors would be denied a trip to the big show. And right behind Banks stood Billy Williams, whose No. 26 would join Banks's No. 14 as the first retired uniform numbers in Cubs history.

Williams, in fact, became my favorite Cub. And little did I know in 1969 that 30 years later, in 1999, on a warm spring evening in Los Angeles, Billy Williams would amble up to a photographer's well at Dodger Stadium and say to me, "Hey, No. 26, would you get me some peanuts when that peanut man comes around?" Knowing that the "peanut man," wasn't coming around anytime soon, I wondered how to get Billy Williams his peanuts. I eyed the Dodgers' dugout on the opposite side of the field knowing the home team has bags of peanuts placed on their bench by the clubhouse attendants. With the national anthem beginning and no time to waste, a bolt of lightning

The Hall of Fame plaque of Chicago Cubs legend Ernie Banks (left), an instrumental player toward the team's quest to win a championship during the late '60s and early '70s along with Billy Williams. Williams, shown here wearing a smile brought about after visiting with Cubs fans during a team practice in Arizona, wore the Cubs uniform as a player and coach through five decades, longer than any player in the franchise's history.

Billy Williams, a six-time All Star outfielder with the Chicago Cubs from 1959-1974, played on highly talented Cubs teams that never made it to the post-season. His performance on the field and devotion to the Chicago Cubs is honored at Wrigley Field with a flag displaying his retired number 26, and a plaque along the Cubs "Walk of Fame."

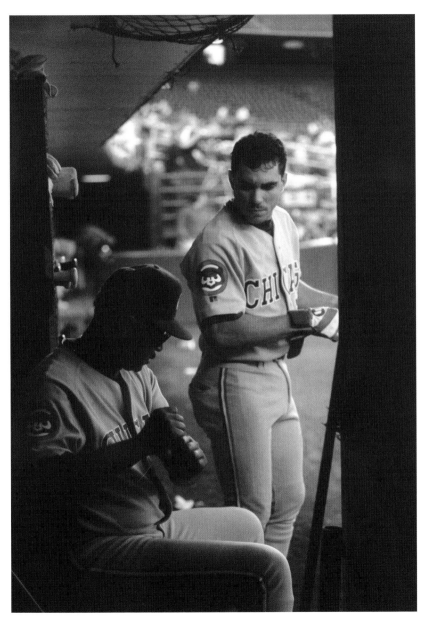

Following his induction to the National Baseball Hall of Fame in 1987, Billy Williams continued his association with the Cubs as a batting instructor and coach for 15 seasons. During the 2002 season he traded in the uniform he wore as a player and a coach for 31 seasons to become an executive member of the Cubs front office. Here, Williams is shown on the field and in the dugout coaching Cubs infielder Ray Sanchez.

Cubs pitching legend Ferguson Jenkins career included nine seasons with the Cubs teams of the late '60s and early '70s, as well as two seasons in the early '80s before his retirement as a player. Jenkins returned to the Cubs during the late '90s to wear the uniform again as a pitching coach.

ignited my path as I sprinted behind home plate, crossed the diamond, and landed in the Dodgers dugout. "Billy Williams wants some peanuts," I stated matter-of-factly. With looks of surprise on the faces of the Dodgers players, one of them handed me a large sack of peanuts. "Thanks," I said quickly. "He asked me to tell you that he'll pay you back later." Laughter erupted from the Dodgers dugout as I repeated my sprint back toward the Cubs bench and headed for Billy Williams. Tossing him the peanuts I warned him, "You better eat them fast. They're contraband." Williams's surprised expression broke into a wide smile. "Ah, there's nothing better than peanuts at the old ball park," he commented while tearing open the bag. "And Dodgers peanuts at that. Okay, No. 26, you've done good. Looks like we're going to win tonight."

Williams nicknamed me with his own number, 26, because when we first met in 1993 I told him I chose to wear his number during my years of playing softball. I also shared with him my special memory of a home run he hit during a Hall of Fame game in 1971. Sitting in the right-field bleachers of Doubleday Field, I wasn't fazed that the Cleveland Indians won the game, because Billy Williams hit a home run that landed right at my feet. "Did you get the ball?" Williams asked me decades later. "No, I didn't because it hit the floor of the bleachers and ricocheted away," I told him.

Over the seasons I documented the Cubs fans on their eternal journey, Billy Williams became a friend. We always found a few minutes to sit and talk, sometimes about that season and sometimes about years gone by.

"When the Cubs went into another rebuilding in the early '70s," explained Williams, "I had to make a decision. I could've ended my career with the Cubs, but I wanted to go to the World Series. At the end of the '74 season I went home and told my wife, 'I'm going hunting. Nobody knows where I am.' And I went into the woods and thought about what to do because the Oakland A's had made me an offer."

Williams's departure completed the wake that began with Banks's retiring after 1971, Santo's crossing town to the White Sox to end his

Ferguson Jenkins Hall of Fame plaque (top) joins Banks and Williams in Cooperstown, where Cubs fans petition the induction of another great Cubs player of the dream team era, Ron Santo.

An All-Star third baseman with the Cubs for thirteen seasons through the '60s and early '70s, Ron Santo returned to the Cubs and continues today as a colorful and popular announcer for Cubs games on WGN-Radio. The Cubs acknowledged his performance by retiring his jersey number 10 at the end of the 2003 season.

career on the South Side in 1974, and Jenkins's moving on to Texas that same year. None of them would ever meet the World Series, but each would return to Chicago again. After two seasons with Oakland, Williams eventually returned to the Cubs as a coach and then as an administrative executive. Ron Santo would return as a radio announcer, Ferguson Jenkins to end his pitching career and again as a pitching coach, and Ernie Banks perennially as the diplomatic "Mr. Cub."

In their return, these Cubs legends bring forward the past not only to the generation of fans who share their broken heart but to generations beyond. They have succeeded in a magnificent way to keep hope and history alive over the past four decades. No, I've never gotten over the heartbreak of '69, but I must say today that sitting with Billy Williams on the bench, chatting with Ron Santo during batting practice, dancing with Fergie Jenkins at the Wrigleyville saloons after the game, and having Ernie Banks walk right by me and say, "Let's play two!" are dreams come true in their own right.

Williams also shared that although they've never gotten over the heartbreak of '69 either, they've also never given up on the dream to witness a Cubs World Series—"whether we see it from the dugout bench, the radio booth, the front office, or sitting in the stands...whenever, however it happens, it's still our dream."

Ron Santo, seated, applauds along with his teammates Ernie Banks (left) and Billy Williams during ceremonies honoring Santo's career with the Cubs when he wore jersey number 10. While retaining hope to one day join Banks, Williams and Jenkins as a member of Baseball's Hall of Fame, Santo continues to devote himself to baseball and the Cubs, despite struggling with complications from diabetes. Living with the disease since his teenage years, Santo has endured amputation of both his legs at the knee in recent years, yet continues on in his work as a radio announcer and ambassador of the Cubs.

CHAPTER 22

Sandberg Sightings

One of my greatest thrills as a Cubs fan was to get close enough to Ryne Sandberg to see that we have the same color eyes—olive green speckled with flecks of amber. I approached him to ask if I could borrow his glove for a photograph. Over the years of watching him play the infield I would notice a glint of sunshine bouncing off his wrist. I realized it was a patch of gold on his glove, marking his expertise as one of the greatest second basemen of all time. But my request to photograph his glove would not be granted for many seasons. "Oh sure," Sandberg replied graciously the first time I asked. "After batting practice I'll be down the line doing my stretches. You can photograph it then." But he mischievously avoided me, and the "glove game" between us went on for years. Finally, in September 1997, when I would see Sandberg for the last time before his retirement, I asked again, and he handed me the glove. Though I was happy to finally photograph his glove, I was a bit saddened at the same time that the game was over.

I was always respectfully aware that the attention Ryne Sandberg received around the baseball field was just plain suffocating to him. An enormously popular player who chose to shun the limelight, Sandberg was a consummate baseball player. Considered quiet and reserved, he had a presence on the baseball field that was equally as commanding and professional. Sandberg would say in his Hall of Fame induction speech in 2005, "I am here today because I'm told I played the game a certain way, the way it was supposed to be played."

Ryne Sandberg, member of 10 National League All-Star teams, was a superstar mainstay at second base for the Chicago Cubs from the early '80s to the late '90s while guiding the team into two post-seasons. Joining the Baseball Hall of Fame in 2005 (left), Sandberg's induction speech will forever reverberate the concept of playing the game of baseball "the way it is supposed to be played... the natural way..."

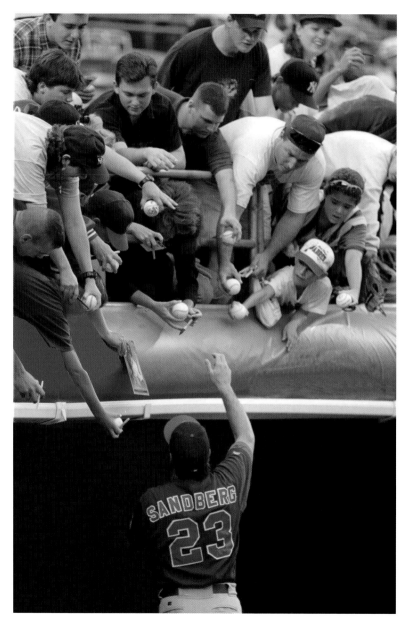

And play the game he did: a 10-time All-Star, nine-time Gold Glove winner, eight-time Silver Slugger winner, owner of the record for most home runs by a second baseman, record holder with 123 consecutive errorless games, 1984 Most Valuable Player, and Cubs escort to the playoffs twice, 1984 and 1989. It's fair to say that when Cubs general manager Dallas Green tacked Sandberg onto a trade with Philadelphia that headlined Larry Bowa and Ivan DeJesus, the baby got "thrown in" with the bath water.

Sandberg ascended rapidly to stardom, hitting a high gear by 1984 and fitting perfectly into the nucleus of a young and successful Cubs team. That year, the Cubs won the National League East, and Sandberg won the Most Valuable Player award. As Cubs fans prepared for their first postseason since 1945, it appeared that Sir Galahad had finally arrived to pull the sword from the stone. In fact, a World Series seemed imminent after the Cubs won their first two playoff games in Chicago and flew with high hopes to San Diego, needing to win one more game from the Padres.

And, as if there were…a curse, or something…the Cubs lost the next three games, with the crushing blow being a ground ball that skipped through the legs of Cubs first baseman Leon Durham. This critical error, combined with a clutch performance by Padre Steve Garvey, sent the Cubs home "waiting for next year." I suppose 1969 rendered me somewhat capable of rising above the sinking feeling of loss and heartache. But the experience of gut-wrenching misfortune was new to my 15-year-old brother, Steve, and he was devastated. If I remember right he ran away from home for at least a full day. My heart ached for him, and I shared his feelings, yet I also knew that one day this too would pass.

Whatever was to blame for the Cubs' collapse in 1984, Ryne Sandberg was not part of it. In fact, he remained something to show as the Cubs continued to evolve as an exciting team into the

After returning from a temporary retirement beginning June, 1994 through the 1995 season, Ryne Sandberg took his final bows as a player at the end of the 1997 season. Here, Sandberg signs autographs for fans in San Diego (left), during his last pass through the major leagues as one of the greatest second basemen of all time. Fans will remember Sandberg as an ultimate multi-tool player: one who excelled in running with speed, hitting with power, fielding with finesse, and throwing with accuracy.

second half of the decade. Talent flowed into the organization from the Cubs farm system adding young stars such as Dwight Smith, Jerome Walton, Shawon Dunston, Greg Maddux, and Mark Grace. When veteran star Andre Dawson joined the team to raise the bar on the youth movement, he and Sandberg quickly led the parade of young Cubs to another postseason in 1989.

But we weren't back for long. The '89 pennant series with the San Francisco Giants seemed doomed from the beginning as a devastating earthquake in the Bay Area jolted the joy out of the atmosphere. Just as suddenly it seemed that Cubs pitchers couldn't find the plate, and usually reliable hitters couldn't find the ball. The Cubs overall seemed all shook up. Once again, we would be waiting for next year, and this time my brother threw his TV set out the window of his fraternity house. Meanwhile, Ryne Sandberg would shelve a regret that became everlasting in his playing career with the Cubs—he would not bring a World Series to Chicago.

The future would see Sandberg retire prematurely in 1994, only to return in 1996 and retire again at the end of 1997. While some thought the early retreat might harm his chances to reach the Hall of Fame, his accomplishments and respect for the game brought him to Cooperstown in 2005, and the Cubs retired his No. 23 to fly next to Banks, Williams, and Santo at Wrigley Field.

Proving his stated love of baseball, Sandberg returned to the Cubs organization in 2007 as the manager of the Peoria Chiefs, a Cubs Single A minor league club. In Peoria, located three hours from Chicago, Sandberg joins young Cubs prospects on long bus rides to places like Appleton, Wisconsin, where the temperature on an early April day is 30 degrees and snowing. Before every game he is seen signing autographs for 15–20 minutes with the local fans and meeting young men who tell him they were named "Ryne" because of him. Will he turn the bus toward Chicago one day and bring the Cubs to a World Series as their manager? "Well…," the Cubs fans say, "wouldn't that be…just perfect."

Ryne Sandberg's preparation before each play at second base was a repetition of motion beginning with a crouch to pick up a bit of dirt with his fingers to gain traction on his throwing hand for double plays at the bag, such as this one putting out the LA Dodgers Bett Butler. The Cubs retired Sandberg's jersey number 23 prior to his Hall of Fame induction to Cooperstown in 2005. He achieved nine gold gloves and eight silver slugger awards during his fifteen seasons with the Cubs.

CHAPTER 23

Three Strikes to an Out

When the Cubs failed to resign pitcher Greg Maddux he departed the Cubs in favor of the Atlanta Braves where he continued to evolve into one of the great superstars of the game.

The lost postseasons of '84 and '89 brought Cubs fans to an expectation and myself to a realization. Despite these recent setbacks, the 1990s arrived with reasonable promise. After all, the division-winning team of yesteryear remained intact, and perhaps a few critical additions would bring them beyond what they'd already accomplished.

However, the 1993 season would kick off with three strikes against the Cubs. Two important pieces of yesteryear, Andre Dawson and Greg Maddux, each signed contracts with new teams. While Dawson would leave some of his best years at Wrigley Field, the young Maddux would bring his best years to Atlanta. In each case, Cubs fans felt a loss of presence and talent with these key departures. To top this off, Ryne Sandberg suffered a broken forearm in spring training and would miss the beginning of the season. Ironically, Opening Day at Wrigley Field featured a victorious Greg Maddux and the Atlanta Braves. It seemed unfair, not to mention weird, and Cubs fans smugly asked, "Greg who?" Even Maddux said he felt dyslexia set in when he had to walk to the visitors dugout instead of to the Cubs.

But, this was just the beginning. A decade that began with excitement continued to change tempo as the 1994 season threatened a players' strike. The Cubs struggled out of the gate, and it appeared Sandberg's injury from a year earlier had stolen his quickness and power at the plate. By mid-June Sandberg cited "personal challenges" in his life, and "loss of enthusiasm" for baseball as he announced an unexpected early retirement. Meanwhile, baseball fans nationwide joined Sandberg as they too began losing interest in the debate over salary caps, revenue

Cubs fans show their difficulty with seeing their former pitching ace, Greg Maddux, wearing an Atlanta Braves
uniform in the opening day game of the 1993 season, as they mockingly question: "Greg Who?" It was an insult
added to the injury of star second baseman Ryne Sandberg a month earlier in spring training. In fact, the year kicked
off a string of bad luck that remained in the air for the next several years.

It was only apparent that something was terribly askew in the game of baseball.

Ryne Sandberg writhes in the pain of a broken forearm after getting hit by a pitch in the early going of spring training, 1993. The injury prevented Sandberg from playing a portion of that season, and many in baseball believe it took away his bat speed and power at the plate.

After struggling to return to the performance he expected of himself, Sandberg would announce an abrupt retirement midway through the next season, 1994, and open the 1995 season signing his autobiography at a Chicago bookstore.

Major League Baseball went dark in August 1994 as an impasse between players and owners began a strike that shut down the remainder of the season. Cubs fans show their displeasure by picketing beneath the Wrigley Field marquis, while Horace Peterson of Chicago (right) carries his own message. The games resumed in late April 1995, but not without baseball having to coax fans back with discounted ticket prices.

Weekday Afternoon Games in April May & Sept.

$15.00	FIELD BOX	$19.00
$11.00	TERR. BOX	$15.00
$11.00	U.D. BOX	$15.00
$8.00	TERR. RES.	$12.00
	U.D. RES.	
$6.00	ADULT	$9.00
$4.00	CHILD	$6.00

50% OFF
April 11th - May 3rd

NO TIPPING
NO REFUNDS OR EXCHANGES
NO CHECKS

Please Check Price, Date & Type
of Tickets BEFORE Leaving Window!

sharing, luxury taxes, and free agency. By August the cloud over baseball turned dark, and the season was called "out." The 1994 World Series was canceled, and the work stoppage caused nearly a full month's delay to the next season.

The damage was done. Many fans lost their passion for the great American pastime, saying that once forced to live without it, they couldn't imagine returning with the same love for the game. Some fans claimed they would never return again, while others found minor league baseball to be a refreshing alternative.

Not certain if baseball could recover from this tailspin, I decided to cover an ambiguous Opening Day at Wrigley Field in late April 1995. Before I left my hotel for the ballpark that morning I received a startling phone call. My former boss and mentor at the L.A. Times, Jim Wilson, had passed away suddenly of a heart attack. Feeling completely deflated, I looked out the hotel window at drizzle falling from a steel gray sky. Despite my sudden sadness, an inspiration persisted deep within me as I heard Wilson say, "Go out there and find the magic."

Magic? The sidewalk beneath the Wrigley Field marquis was quiet except for a few major league umpires carrying strike signs. The generally busy ticket windows were empty except for signs advertising a 50 percent discount. A handful of Cubs fans joined the umpires with their own signs of protest, while others gathered in small groups at the bars around Wrigleyville. The atmosphere inside the stadium was equally dismal, with just a paltry crowd of fans willing to pass the picket lines and take a seat for the ballgame. Although I looked in all the usual places, I could not find the magic. It was only apparent that something was terribly askew in the game of baseball, until a thought struck me: I wondered if the Cubs fans who traditionally gather on Opening Day to "pass the Drambuie" were in their usual gathering spot. Taking this glimmer of hope along I hurried my way toward Sheffield Avenue and, sure enough, there they were exchanging laughter and a Drambuie bottle among themselves. I found the encounter to be heartening, seeing it as an ember of the faith that would spark again one day into a roaring flame. I learned that even on this damp, cold, and dreary day there was magic to be found, after all.

"Baseball makes us stronger," they told me. "You've got to believe."

The strike year of 1994 began a series of losing seasons for the Cubs that wouldn't turn around completely until 1998. Trying to help the Cubs bust their slump during these years, Sam Sianas of the Billy Goat Tavern visits Wrigley Field (left) to make one of his occasional attempts to reverse the curse of the Billy Goat. Meanwhile, Cubs fan Linda Medo, a Chicago native who resides in New Jersey, shows off a newspaper photo of herself cheering the Cubs through a losing streak while the team was on the road at Shea Stadium.

CHAPTER 24

S-O-S-A Mania

Who knew that baseball would rise from the ashes of '94 and '95 to reach a perfect moment within a few years? On June 20, 1998, Sammy Sosa launched a monstrous home run that reached a rooftop across Waveland Avenue and sent a clear message to the world: Baseball is back! The miraculous season of '98 would go down in history as "the Great Home Run Chase," with Sosa of the Cubs squaring off with Mark McGwire of the St. Louis Cardinals.

And the winner was…baseball! With a resolute rebound from the darkened seasons of its recent past, major league baseball suddenly set attendance records across the board. The Cubs played before sold-out stadiums at home and on the road. Everyone wanted to see Sosa hit one more. By September the streets of Wrigleyville overflowed with mania as huge crowds gathered at the corner of Waveland and Kenmore in hopes of snagging a Sosa home run. The real ballhawks were distraught over losing their privacy, but hysteria had taken hold as every day became more surprising.

Sammy Sosa came to the Cubs to begin the 1992 season with an undisciplined swing and an unfettered conscience. In time both would change. Touted as possessing "untapped potential," the young and wild Sosa was determined to succeed, but he admitted years later that he was trying too hard, expecting to hit two home runs in one at-bat. With each passing season Sosa evolved as a respected power hitter and was recognized and embraced by fans nationwide for an ebullient attitude that brought joy and passion back to baseball. By 1998 he emerged as one of the game's greatest home-run sluggers, and his ascension brought him to a level of popularity that would transcend the Cubs, transcend baseball, and for a time be larger than life itself. Though McGwire won the race with an amazing 70 home runs to Sosa's 66, it was Sosa who was named Most Valuable Player in baseball and who became an international icon.

Despite the 1998 season ending with the Cubs being swept by Atlanta in the postseason, there was an afterglow in Chicago that winter named Sammy Sosa. His presence swirled through the city like the wind, gracing buses, trains, billboards, and even the sides of five-story buildings with his personage. He would

Cubs super slugger Sammy Sosa finds himself surrounded by a sea of media, and increased expectations of performance, during the "Great Homerun Chase" of 1998 between Sosa and St. Louis Cardinals Mark McGwire. Cubs fans cheering on Sosa in the Wrigley Field bleachers (left) are Tim Rerick, Kory Futa, Brett Godsey and Kevin Sechowski, all from Purdue University in South Bend, Indiana.

As Sammy Sosa soared to spectacular heights he lost the ability to enjoy carefree moments such as a good laugh with his teammates before games. Instead, the anticipation of his next homerun grew among Cubs fans. They let him know by hanging his native Dominican Republic flag around the ballpark, wearing his jersey to the games, and encouraging him to hit a homer square at their chest - such as the message worn on a T-shirt by Lucas Devoe, an eleven-year-old Cubs fan (1998).

Whether at Wrigley Field or other major league ballparks visited by Sosa, baseball fans of all varieties joined the escalating mania of the homerun chase between Sosa and McGwire. Here, Cubs fan Glenda Dennison of San Diego (left) is joined by throngs of fans at Jack Murphy Stadium wanting to see Sosa hit yet another homerun. Sosa did hit number 63 on this night, and it was a dramatic grand slam. Meanwhile, Chicago became enthralled with their superhero and for a time his image graced every corner of the city, including this larger-than-life mural painted on all four sides of a huge building in the city's warehouse district and visible to traffic passing along the adjacent expressway.

HIS ASCENSION BROUGHT HIM TO A LEVEL THAT WOULD TRANSCEND THE CUBS,
TRANSCEND BASEBALL, AND FOR A TIME BE LARGER THAN LIFE ITSELF.

return in the spring to an enormous expectation: "Do it again, Sam." And he did. His curtain call never ended, such as his heroic home run in the Cubs' first game after the September 11, 2001, tragedy. Expecting a magical moment, Cubs first-base coach Billy Williams had a small American flag in hand with Sosa at bat. On cue, Sosa launched the ball into the Wrigley Field bleachers and took the flag from Williams as he rounded first base, waving it high above his head for the remainder of his home-run trot. The nation was proud, and Sammy Sosa was proud, that a "shoe-shine boy" from the Dominican Republic stood for our country's undivided belief—in America all are free to pursue their dreams.

Yet, within Sosa's rise to immense stardom there was a parallel demise of his personal joy of the game. Gone were the days when Sammy could saunter onto the field during batting practice, joke around with teammates, sign autographs for fans. Media attention became so intense on Sosa that missing batting practice became routine because he had to do pregame press conferences. And when he did find time for batting practice he had to make his way through a wall of media just to get to the field. Beyond this, even batting practice held expectations for Sosa's performance as audiences gathered to see him hit home runs in what became "Sammy's pregame show."

On June 3, 2003, the show became a shame when Sosa swung at a ball that broke his bat and revealed cork. Sosa was ejected from the game, and Major League Baseball went on to confiscate and test 81 of his other bats, including five sent in past years to the Hall of Fame. All were found to be clean, and Sosa stated that the corked bat was one he used only in batting practice, to put on his "show" for the crowds, and he accidentally used it during a regulation game. Whatever the explanation, Sosa's reputation and fortunes would never be the same. The corked bat contributed to a fall from grace, as the once-proud city of Chicago looked away.

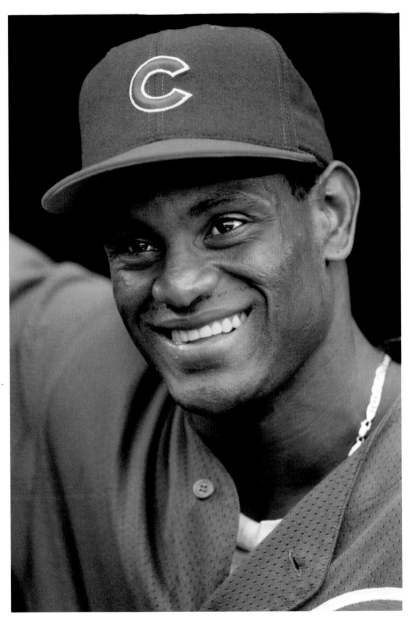

Rumors of steroid use followed Sosa after the Cubs traded him to the Baltimore Orioles before the 2005 season. Observers remained suspicious as his athletic skill fell into a noticeable slump with Baltimore, though he never tested positive for any performance-enhancing drugs. After one season the Orioles released Sosa's contract, and it appeared his baseball days were history, leaving the game just 12 long balls shy of 600 for his career, with 545 of those home runs hit in a Chicago Cubs uniform, a franchise record that may never be broken. It seemed a terribly unfortunate ending to a story with such glorious highlights, ironically from a man whose mantra was "it's not about how you start, but it's all about how you finish."

After taking one year completely away from baseball, Sosa decided to take his mantra to heart and returned to baseball in 2007 with the dedication to surpass the 600 home-run mark with the Texas Rangers. Intending for his final effort to gain him a positive finish, Sosa's mantra might end up being more like this: it's not about how you fall, but it's all about how you get up, dust yourself off, and carry on.

Nicholas Cien (left), a young San Diego Padres fan in 1998, is compelled to thank Sammy Sosa for the good times brought about by the great homerun chase. Though Mark McGwire's 70 homeruns outdistanced Sosa's 66, the intense excitement and interest of the two players performances did help to bring baseball fans back from the down years following the '94 strike.

CHAPTER 25

A Saving Grace

Chicago Cubs first baseman Mark Grace bonded with Cubs fans through his 13 seasons at Wrigley Field becoming one of the most popular players to ever wear the Cubs uniform.

A decade that began with great trumpeting, dropped to a low note, rose to a high note, and concluded by floating off-key into a new millennium. After the magical season of 1998 there was no encore other than another showdown between Sosa and McGwire. With headlines that read "SOSA HITS TWO, BUT CUBS STILL LOSE," the challenge for the team became how to win more games than Sammy hit home runs. Some suggested that baseball was beginning to turn into a game of individual heroics. Winning the game didn't seem to matter anymore, as long as someone hit a home run. And for the record, from June 1999 through the 2000 season, the Cubs would lose more games than any other major league team. Yet, throughout the decade the Chicago Cubs had a "saving grace," a player considered to be a Cubs fan in uniform, the guy that did everything else while Sammy was hitting home runs. And when the curtain closed on the 20th century it was Mark Grace who emerged to take a bow for registering more hits in the past decade than any other player in the game.

Beyond his outstanding performance with the Cubs from 1988 through 2000, Mark Grace brought a charisma to the ball field that uplifted players and fans alike. Considered by many to be the modern-day "Mr. Cub," his never-say-die attitude was infectious and unquenchable, even during the worst of times. While certainly proud of his four Gold Gloves along with the most hits and most doubles in the decade, Grace really only cared about one thing: Cubs win! I congratulated Grace the day after a game against the Dodgers when he went 5 for 5. "Great game last night, Mark," I

Beyond his great talent and intense desire to win as a player, Mark Grace's down-to-earth and fun loving personality connected with Cubs fans to the point where they considered him one of their own. Grace's presence in the Cubs uniform was always a positive, through both the thick and the thin. With dedication to the Cubs that spanned the decade, Grace is shown above in 1991 (inset), and 1999.

Mark Grace distinguished himself by becoming the major league player with the "most hits in the '90s." He added four gold gloves to his credit during the decade as well. He proudly admires a gold glove received at the beginning of the 1993 season (right) for his outstanding fielding performance during 1992.

said as he was walking past me toward the batting cage. Looking straight ahead, and without breaking stride, he responded, "We lost."

Always trying something to get his team geared up, Grace was a veritable cheerleader who coaxed players out of slumps by offering them money for hits and runs batted in. He abandoned his incentive program after a while because he found he owed himself the most money. Though sometimes criticized for a renegade style, he remained steadfast in his objective to help the Cubs win in any way he could. During the 2000 season he even shaved his head to help break a slump, and he ended up inciting half the team to go bald. Even with the striking blond hair gone and the fun-loving grin fading, Grace's piercing green eyes remained focused on the goal of bringing his beloved Cubs to a World Series. He said once if they ever won it he would be the first Cubs fan to storm the streets of Wrigleyville. "I'll be out there jumping on top of cars with the rest of them," he joked.

Desiring to end an illustrious and passionate career in a Cubs uniform, Grace asked for a multiyear contract at the end of the decade but was only offered a one-year extension. Many feared that the Cubs would not re-sign Grace after the 2000 season, and they were right. Like Ron Santo, another player who wore his love for the Cubs on his sleeve, Grace would play 13 years for the Cubs, before signing with a new team. But at least he didn't leave the North Side for the White Sox, though he would admit that toward the end he nearly signed with the White Sox, Cleveland Indians, and St. Louis Cardinals. "But I belong in a Cubs uniform," he said in the end. "Anybody who knows me, and knows the Cubs, knows that."

It was with a heavy heart, therefore, that Mark Grace changed uniforms by signing with the Arizona Diamondbacks in 2001. And the city of Chicago grieved the loss of a player who fit into their crowd and their culture like a glove. "How could we ever have a party without him?" Cubs fans asked. It just didn't seem right. But Grace would end up at a party after all, when the Arizona Diamondbacks marched to a World Series victory in his first season with the new team. "How does it feel," the media asked him, "after trying for all those years in Chicago and now bringing a World Series to Phoenix in one season?" As always Grace's remarks reflected the feelings of Cubs fans everywhere: "It's bittersweet."

"But I belong in a Cubs uniform, anybody who knows me and knows the Cubs, knows that."

Mark Grace is joined by Cubs catcher Jody Reed, outfielder Brant Brown and pitcher Kerry Wood as part of the "bald brigade," a head shaving tactic incited by Grace to motivate the Cubs to make a late season push during the 2000 season. While the Cubs fell short of the playoffs that year, and would in fact lose Grace to free agency at its end, his devotion and passion was always evident, such as this game-ending embrace to Cubs pitcher Reuben Quevedo.

CHAPTER 26

When Hope & History Rhyme

As the new millennium unfolds, the Chicago Cubs and their fans continue to march toward a destiny of desire while holding an unfulfilled dream close to heart. With the dawning of the 2008 season they will reach the dubious distinction of passing through 100 years without a World Series victory. And the question remains, "When will the Fat Lady sing our song?" Yet, we know there are simply not answers to all things in life, and we believe the mystery is part of the enduring magic that makes it all worthwhile. With that accepted we keep our dream alive with faith, and remind one another to never say never. And when we are asked, "What is it about Cubs fans that keep them coming back for more?" perhaps we should reveal the essence of it all: we've enjoyed the passage of time.

We've enjoyed each and every day. We've enjoyed each and every season. And we've enjoyed every player to wear the uniform, and every team that toiled toward victory.

And we've enjoyed each other. Through the decades the players retired, resigned, and were traded. But some of them would choose to return and become one of us. Because when all is said and done, we are the Chicago Cubs. We have been for more than 100 years, and we hope to be always. It's all we want. There is nothing else. We're not going to change our hats. We're Cubs fans, and that's it.

Do we want the Cubs to win? You bet we do! Does it spoil our fun if the Cubs lose? Absolutely not…well, maybe it does a little bit. It is true that as Cubs fans we live with a tension of opposites. While we want the Cubs to win the World Series, we do not want things to change, because we truly enjoy the way things are. Often the question is asked, if the Cubs win the World Series will it change everything? I liken this question to being asked, if you won a multimillion-dollar lottery would your life be different?

Cubs fan Rodney Marshall of Galesburg, Illinois passed away without his dream coming true: to witness a Cubs victory in another World Series. Yet, baseball friends decorate his headstone with Cubs memorabilia before their trips to Wrigley Field each season, noting that they carry his dream in their heart. Likewise, all Cubs fans carry on the tradition of passing forward their love of the Chicago Cubs to younger generations and beyond.

The first decade of the new century brought a focus on three young pitchers whose talents combined effectively in one season, 2003, to bring the Cubs within five outs of a World Series appearance. The team and its fans remain waiting for the full potential of Kerry Wood (above), Mark Prior (far right), and Carlos Zambrano (right) to blossom. Repeated injury has sidelined both Wood and Prior throughout their early years with the Cubs, while Carlos Zambrano emerged as the star and the workhorse of the staff.

THE CHICAGO CUBS AND THEIR FANS
CONTINUE TO MARCH TOWARD A DESTINY
OF DESIRE... AND THE QUESTION REMAINS,
"WHEN WILL THE FAT LADY SING OUR SONG?"

As Rodney Marshall lies quietly beneath a headstone in Galesburg, Illinois, life goes on in this small town in the southwestern corner of the state. Rodney was born a Cubs fan, and his childhood friends visit his grave on special days to decorate it with Cubs pennants and American flags. Rodney fought in the Vietnam War, and he died in 1994 at age 45 from complications of Agent Orange. Like so many before him, and so many after him, Rodney's life would come and go without realizing the dream of seeing the Cubs win the World Series. But his friends say that growing up rooting for the Cubs, traveling together to games at Wrigley Field over the years, left them each with memories knitted into the very fabric of their life. In this way, they tell me, Rodney lives within us, and we carry his dream in our hearts every day. It's not so different, they say, from passing the dream on to the next generation. It's larger than any one of us, but it's a part of all of us.

Jack Fleischer of Chicago chooses to show his devotion to the Cubs with an embroidered yamaka, while a Cubs player displays his faith with a large, gold cross.

THERE ARE SIMPLY NOT ANSWERS TO ALL THINGS IN LIFE, AND WE BELIEVE THE MYSTERY IS PART OF THE ENDURING MAGIC THAT MAKES IT ALL WORTHWHILE.

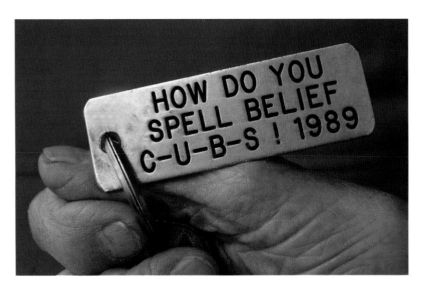

As Wrigley Field lies quietly beneath another blanket of winter snow it waits for a moment to share with you. It is you who brings the life into each new season. On Opening Day every player on the field might be different from the year before. But you are still the same. I can find you where you were last year, and where you'll be again next year. I made this journey wanting to get to know you, because we share the same dream. I traveled by plane, train, bus, and cab to be with you. I walked countless miles through city streets with a backpack of camera gear rubbing the skin off my shoulders so I could photograph you and talk with you. Some of you became friends that will last my lifetime, but all of you became the time of my life.

How many next years await us? None of us knows the answer. We only know that our promise renews with the New Year during the next Cubs Convention, our hopes return in Arizona with the next spring training, our dreams come alive through the next season at Wrigley Field, while our love of the Chicago Cubs is forever.

And one day, when hope and history rhyme, the Fat Lady will sing along with us. In the meanwhile we know that what counts in life is not the destination…but only the journey.

See you next year…

With more than one way to express their faith, some Cubs fans show off engraved key chains while others proudly display their "Die-Hard Cubs Fan Club" card, a fraternity of Cubs fans started by television personality and Cubs fan Bryant Gumble. This card states it belongs to Jack Carlson, a Cubs fan since 1932.

Toward the end of another season, the Cubs announce the dates of next year's Cubs Convention on the marquis at the corner of Clark and Addison while a street musician bids Wrigley Field a farewell with his saxophone to remind us that the beat goes on...